Historic **Armenia**
After 100 Years
ANI, KARS, AND THE SIX PROVINCES OF WESTERN ARMENIA

HISTORIC ARMENIA THROUGHOUT THE AGES

Despite centuries of changing frontiers, the heart of the Armenian nation has always been located on the Armenian Plateau—the highland region that extends from Kilikia to the Caucasus.

Istanbul

Ankar

TURKEY

Anatolia

Mediterranean Sea

Empire of Tigran the Great (95 - 55 BC)

Kilikia Armenia (1080 - 1375)

The First Armenian Republic (1918 - 1920)

Republic of Armenia (1991 - Date)

Historic Armenia

Armenia as Proposed by U.S. President Wilson

Artsakh (Karabakh) Republic (1991 - Date)

Black Sea

Caucasus Mountains

Lake Sevan

Kars ●   **Yerevan**
        ● Ani   ◎

Erzincan ●   Stepanakert
                                      ◎

Yozgat ●

Erzerum ●

Armenian Plateau

● Sebastia

Arax

Kesaria ●

Lesser
Armenia

Aratsani

● Palu   Mush ●
                        Lake Van
                Bitlis ●   ● Van
Kharpert ●

● Malatya

Lake Urmia

Diyarbakir ●

K I L I K I A

G R E A T E R   A R M E N I A

IRAN

● Adana

SYRIA

Tigris

LEBANON

Euphrates

IRAQ

0   300 km

0   100   200 mi

Courtesy of Robert H. Hewsen

Historic **Armenia**
After 100 Years
ANI, KARS, AND THE SIX PROVINCES OF WESTERN ARMENIA

Text and Photography by Matthew Karanian

Houstian Hayotsian Barsoian

Ardemis Dikranian Karanian

FOR MY GRANDMOTHERS

THEY SURVIVED THE ARMENIAN
GENOCIDE AND BECAME PART OF THE
FOUNDATION UPON WHICH OUR
NATION WAS REBUILT

A building in the former Armenian district of Zara

Mayrig

Zara was Mayrig's hometown.

That's all I needed to know, to know that I had to travel to Zara.

Mayrig was the Matriarch of my family, my grandmother. She died before I was born, but I got to know her through her daughter, my Mother.

Mom would tell me stories about Mayrig when I was a child. The stories continued into my adulthood and they almost always ended the same way. They ended with my Mom telling me how much she misses Mayrig. Mayrig, who had passed away more than 50 years ago, was still missed.

This was all I really ever needed to know about Mayrig. Fifty years later. And her 90-year old daughter still missed her to tears.

I did learn a few details about Mayrig's life, however.

I learned that she lived near Sebastia in the Western Armenia town of Zara with her husband and children until the summer of 1915.

I learned that she and her children watched in horror one evening while a group of townspeople hurled rocks at her husband, their father, until he was dead.

And I learned that this grieving widow and her five children were then deported from their home.

Three of her five children, Barkev, Herepsime, and Azniv, died during the deportation. A fourth child, 7-year old Hagop, was kidnapped by a Kurdish family. Only Mayrig and Yeghishe, Mayrig's strongest and oldest son, survived the death march. Before the year was over, everyone else who Mayrig knew from her life in Zara—family and inlaws, neighbors and friends—would be dead.

Then, for three years, the story grows murky. Three years later, she and her sole surviving child Yeghishe ended up in Adana, on the Mediterranean coast.

They had walked 500 kilometers from the north of Anatolia at Sebastia, to its southernmost tip at Adana. It took them three years, but they walked.

What happened during those three years? How can a mother and her child walk for three years? These questions, and countless more, were devoured, unanswered, by the abyss of the holocaust.

Mayrig and Yeghishe stayed in Adana for a few years. Mayrig worked as a nurse's aid. Eventually, with the assistance of American missionaries in 1922, they were able to escape to the US. They settled first in Massachusetts, and then in Rhode Island.

Mayrig was beautiful, and when the Armenian men in her new hometown of Pawtucket learned that this Armenian refugee had arrived from the homeland, they courted her. Mayrig sent them away. No, she would kindly tell them. I've already been married. I have already had a life. I'm too old now. I won't start another family.

But eventually she did.

Mayrig, who had been born in the town of Zara as Houstian Hayotsian, married my grandfather, a man who had traveled to the US from nearby Sebastia just one year before the genocide. His name was Oskean Barsoian. Together they had two more children, first Agnes, who was given the same name as another of Mayrig's daughters who had been killed in the genocide; and then Harry. Agnes would become my Mom. Harry would become my Godfather.

Mayrig loved America. She thanked God that she had a home here, and that she was safe. But Mayrig also loved her home in Zara.

I wish I could be a bird, she would tell my Mom when Mom was a little girl and believed, as all little girls do, that wishes come true. I wish I could be a bird for just one day, so I could fly over my home in Zara and see it just one more time.

And so I traveled to Zara.

The journey was long. By one measure it took me two days. By another measure, it had taken 99 years. Mayrig had left Zara 99 years ago, and until my visit, no one from her family had ever returned.

After 99 years, I imagined that Mayrig's wish had come true. I imagined that she had seen her hometown one last time, through her grandchild's eyes.

And after a lifetime of having only heard about Mayrig, I imagined that I had finally seen her, too.

9

Cover Photo

Ktuts Monastery
on Ktuts Island, Lake Van

Page 1 Photo

Ararat Valley, Republic of Armenia

Published in the USA by the Stone Garden Press

Copyright © 2015 Matthew Karanian

TEXT
Text © 2015 Matthew Karanian

PHOTOGRAPHS
Photographs © 2015 Matthew Karanian, unless indicated otherwise
Photograph p. 73 © 2015 Bared Maronian
Photographs pp. 60, 71, 148 © 2015 Samvel Karapetyan

MAPS
Reference Maps © 2015 Robert Hewsen, unless indicated otherwise
Map of Historic Armenia (inside back cover) © 2013 Karanian Family Trust

DESIGN AND CREATIVE DIRECTION
Harut Genjoyan, AlphaGraph, LLC, Glendale, California | www.AlphaGraphCG.com

Printed in the United States of America
10 9 8 7 6 5 4 3 2 1

LIBRARY OF CONGRESS CONTROL NUMBER 2014920224
ISBN 978-0-9672120-6-7

The publisher and author are solely responsible for the content of this book. They have made every effort to make the information in this book as accurate as possible, but they accept no responsibility for any loss, injury, or inconvenience sustained by anyone using this book.

About This Guide

This book is the first-ever guide to cultural sites of the vast and ancient Armenian homeland that is located in today's Turkey. The text describes the history and culture of the Armenian monuments and artifacts that are still present. The photography documents the current condition of these ancient sites.

In many cases, historic images from 100 years ago are included. These images illustrate the once magnificent condition of some of the Armenian churches, monasteries, and towns that are now either in ruins or that were razed after 1915. There are many non-Armenian sites in this part of historic Armenia, too, but they are beyond the scope of this book.

The six Armenian provinces of the Ottoman Empire that comprised **Western Armenia** are featured according to their 1915 borders. The **Eastern Armenian** region of **Kars**, which was located within the Russian Empire in 1915 and which had become part of the first Armenian Republic in 1918, is also included. Each of these regions is located within today's Turkey.

The regional boundaries from 1915 have been used in order to create a snapshot of historic Armenia from that year, which is the year that marked both the start of the Armenian holocaust and the end of the 3,000-year habitation of Armenians in their homeland.

Other regions of historic Armenia, such as Kilikia (Giligia), Javakhk, and Nakhichevan, are beyond the scope of this volume. The Republic of Armenia and the Republic of Artsakh (The Nagorno Karabakh Republic), which are both free and independent, are featured separately by the author in **Armenia and Karabakh: The Stone Garden Travel Guide.**

At time of research, most regions covered in this book were peaceful, and the risk of civil disturbance or war was low. The greatest risk of harm to travelers at time of research was along the border region near Syria and Iraq, which is located south of the regions of Diyarbakir and Van. Conditions change over time, however, and readers are advised to carefully evaluate the risks of travel before planning a trip to the region.

If you go, **suggested itineraries** are provided at the end of each chapter. **GPS** (**Global Positioning System**) coordinates have been provided for sites that are off the beaten path and which would be difficult to locate using conventional directions. GPS coordinates have not been listed for well-known sites that are easy to locate, such as, for example, major cities and towns.

Sponsors

Edward Misserlian of *San Francisco, California*, pledged generous support for this publication during its research and planning. This early financial support launched the project. **Agnes Karanian** of *New Britain, Connecticut*, provided a significant gift that assured the project would be completed. The cost to design and print this book was also supported by generous donations from several other individuals. Thank you to the following major sponsors:

Assemblyman Khatchik H. Achadjian, *San Luis Obispo, California*
George and Joyce Aghjayan, *Westminster, Massachusetts*
Richard P. Ahronian, *Fresno, California*
Sarkis and Rebecca Berberian, *Glendale, California*
Ken and Gloria Hachikian, *Lake Forest, Illinois*
Simon and Maral Hasserjian, *Thornhill, Ontario*
Nora Hovsepian, *Encino, California*
Charles G. Karanian, *New Britain, Connecticut*
George K. Karanian, *Suffield, Connecticut*
Elisa Kekejian, *Montreal, Quebec*
Sarhad Melkonian, *Mahwah, New Jersey*
Vahe and Nora Yacoubian, *Los Angeles, California*
Robert Mugar Yacubian, *Greenfield, Massachusetts*
Susan Yacubian Klein, *Princeton, New Jersey*
Robert Koligian, Jr., *Fresno, California*
Honorable Tomar Mason, *San Francisco, California*
David and Kathleen Melikian, *Fresno, California*
Michelle Tutelian, *Fresno, California*
Gary Whiteley, *Palm Desert, California*

Table of Contents

An Armenian Airlines jet flies past Mt. Ararat

> *"The struggle of man against power*
> *is the struggle of memory against forgetting."*
>
> —*Milan Kundera*

Foreword

You never forget your first church.

That's what I tell friends who join me on my trips to Western Armenia.

It will likely be in ruins, treasure hunters will have dug holes in it, and vandals will have desecrated it. Yet it will still be standing with defiance and grace.

And—in a poignant reminder that structures, too, can have agency—it will move you, and likely transform you.

But do not forget that around these scarred and ruined remnants of Armenian cultural heritage dotting Turkey, there are people who are an integral part of this land and its history.

They, too, are "remnants." They were referred to as "remnants of the sword," for they were survivors of the Armenian Genocide.

"From the day we opened our eyes, a church stood here," an old woman once told me as we walked past the ruins of the Armenian church in Keserig (Kesrik), in the Kharpert region. "They kept tearing down its walls and taking away the stones until almost nothing remained," she said.

Talk to the "hidden Armenians" who approach you. Talk to their Turkish and Kurdish neighbors. Listen to their stories. Tell them your stories. Explain your connection to the land, the importance of preserving these sites, and the importance of justice.

And remember that not all is hidden or destroyed. There is a small community of Armenians forming in Dikranagerd/Diyarbakir, around the recently-renovated Soorp Giragos Church. Armenian language classes are offered there, and Armenian events—even commemorations of the Armenian Genocide—are now common occurrences in the city.

Diyarbakir has embraced and supported efforts to revive, in small part, its Armenian past. This unique case in Turkey serves as a model of how the country can begin the long process of meaningfully confronting its past.

And Armenians visiting Western Armenian cities and towns are affirming, without even uttering a word, that they are committed to the struggle for truth and justice. An increasing number of locals are getting the message and, in their own way, are joining the struggle.

Daniel Varoujan, the prominent Armenian poet killed during the Genocide, said in one of his poems that he could hear the footsteps of a rose-flooded dawn of victory. From a distance of 100 years, you, dear reader, will probably hear the sounds of the very same footsteps in Western Armenia. They are the footsteps of victory—the victory of memory against forgetting. And they are gradually becoming louder.

———————————— • ————————————

I do not call my own trips to Western Armenia pilgrimages. They are more than what dictionaries define as "a journey to a place associated with someone or something well known or respected." Western Armenia is a place where the "someone or something," hidden or destroyed as it is, still resists erasure. It is still very much alive.

But no matter how you define your trip—tourism, pilgrimage, research, or simply a visit to long lost homes and relatives—there is much that will inform and inspire you in this book.

And if the faces and places of Western Armenia are dear to you, but you're unwilling to visit Turkey, the book that you hold in your hands is the next best thing to being there.

Either way, the journey is worth every penny.

Khatchig Mouradian
February 2015

Mouradian is the Coordinator of the Armenian Genocide Program at the Center for the Study of Genocide and Human Rights at Rutgers University, where he also teaches in the history and sociology departments. He was editor of the Armenian Weekly newspaper from 2007 to 2014.

The Western Armenian foothills of Mt. Ararat

Armenia After 100 Years

Black Sea

Caucasus Mountains

Ankara ◎

Yozgat ●

Sebastia ●

Kesaria ●

Lesser Armenia

Erzincan ●

Erzerum ●

Kars ●

Ani ●

Yerevan ◎

Lake Sevan

Stepanakert ◎

Armenian Plateau

Aratsani

Palu ●

Kharpert ●

Mush ●

Lake Van

Bitlis ●

Van ●

Arax

Malatya ●

Diyarbakir ●

Lake Urmia

KILIKIA

Adana ●

G R E A T E R   A R M E N I A

Mediterranean Sea

IRAN

SYRIA

Tigris

Euphrates

LEBANON

IRAQ

Scale:
0 — 100 — 300 km
0 — 100 — 200 mi

	Empire of Tigran the Great (95 - 55 BC)
	Kilikia Armenia (1080 - 1375)
	The First Armenian Republic (1918 - 1920)
	Republic of Armenia (1991 - Date)
	Historic Armenia
	Armenia as Proposed by U.S. President Wilson
	Artsakh (Karabakh) Republic (1991 - Date)

Courtesy of Robert H. Hewsen

INTRODUCTION

One hundred years after the *Medz Yeghern*, the Armenian homeland remains unknown to many Armenians and non-Armenians alike.

There are many reasons for this. The descendants of the Armenians who survived the *Medz Yeghern*—the **Great Crime**, the **Armenian Genocide**—often choose not to return to their homeland because the memories that they received from their ancestors are so painful.

Others choose not to visit historic Armenia because they believe that their presence there will provide economic support to the people who have wrongfully displaced the native Armenians.

Still others, Armenians and non-Armenians alike, do not travel to historic Armenia because no one has articulated for them a compelling reason to visit. What is there left to learn about, or see, in the Armenian homeland? Hasn't everything been destroyed?

The *Medz Yeghern* began in 1915 and terminated the 3,000-year history of Armenians in their historic homeland. During the past 100 years, the population of Armenians in the land of historic Armenia has been almost completely eliminated. Most of the survivors who returned after 1915 were again compelled to leave. Today, however, there are pockets of hidden Armenian communities that have persisted and that are attempting to express their culture more openly.

These Armenians are sometimes called **hidden Armenians** because for nearly a century they concealed their identities to avoid persecution. They are today beginning to become openly Armenian, and they derive moral support from the Armenians who visit from abroad.

During the one hundred years since 1915, most of the cultural monuments of the Armenian nation in the lands of historic Armenia have been eliminated. Churches and monasteries have been bombed, *khatchkars* have been bulldozed, frescoes have been whitewashed.

But there is still much that remains. Armenian monuments have survived in every region, and are in abundance in places such as Ani and Van. Armenian churches still function in places such as Kesaria (Kayseri) and Diyarbakir. In time, additional churches may be returned to the Armenians. Everything has *not* been destroyed.

By traveling to historic Armenia, visitors signal their interest in these surviving monuments and in Armenian culture and history. The current custodians of Armenian monuments may therefore conclude that an ancient church is more valuable as a tourist destination than as quarry material for, say, a barn.

These are some of the logical and rational reasons for visiting historic Armenia. But the most compelling reason for visiting has nothing to do with either.

Armenians should visit historic Armenia because it is their homeland. No other reason is necessary.

And non-Armenians should visit to celebrate the culture of the world's first Christian state, in a region that is as holy as the Holy Land.

This book introduces the reader, region by region, to the sites of historic Armenia that exist today and that are worth finding, viewing, and enjoying. The sites that are included are the primary sites that should be on your itinerary.

For the pilgrim who is unable to travel to historic Armenia, this book is an alternative to making the journey.

The Armenian Genocide began in 1915, and after one hundred years, it is appropriate to reflect upon all that has been lost in one century. But we should also celebrate, and rally to support, all that still remains. Because whether we witness the passage of one hundred years, or another thousand, this will always be our homeland.

Ani, at the Frontier Between
Western and Eastern Armenia

WESTERN AND EASTERN ARMENIA

Throughout much of its modern history, Armenia has been ruled by foreign powers. This foreign domination has led to the artificial concept of Armenia as consisting of two halves—**Western Armenia** and **Eastern Armenia**.

Western Armenia is the name attributed to the part of Armenia that fell within the suzerainty of the Ottoman Empire. Eastern Armenia is the common name for the part of Armenia that was located within the Russian Empire.

Thus, although there is only one Armenian nation, the designations of Eastern Armenia and Western Armenia are commonly used geographic terms that today describe the lands of the Armenian nation.

Eastern Armenia is sometimes regarded as any of the lands of Armenia that are located east of the modern Republic of Turkey. Such a designation is imprecise, however, because it ignores the history of **Ani** and **Kars**.

Ani and Kars are today controlled by Turkey. But during the periods of modern history when Armenia was ruled by foreign powers, and until 1918, Ani and Kars fell within the suzerainty of Russia. The plains of **Mt. Ararat**, and the mountain itself, were also controlled by Russia. Each of these areas then became, from 1918 until 1920, a part of the independent Republic of Armenia. Hence this area is rightly characterized geographically as Eastern Armenia, despite its current location in Turkey.

The geographic region of Eastern Armenia includes the **Republic of Armenia** and the **Republic of Artsakh** (Nagorno Karabakh), as well as **Nakhichevan** and **Javakhk**.

Western Armenia commonly refers to the six provinces of the Ottoman Empire that were Armenian in 1915. These provinces, or *vilayets*, are **Van**, **Erzerum**, **Bitlis**, **Diyarbakir**, **Kharpert**, and **Sebastia**.

Some Armenians also use the term Western Armenia as shorthand for any historically Armenian areas west of the Republic of Armenia, such as the areas of **Kilikia** (**Giligia**) and any other historically Armenian areas within today's Turkey, such as **Kesaria** (**Kayseri**) in **Cappadocia**.

THE ARMENIAN PLATEAU

The **Armenian Plateau** is a geographic term that describes the land that encompasses much of historic Armenia. This land extends east, beyond Lake Sevan (in today's Republic of Armenia), west, to the edge of Cappadocia, and south, as far as the Taurus Mountains in the area of Bitlis. This is a geographic region, and none of these boundaries is precisely marked.

The Armenian Plateau is sometimes also called the **Armenian Highland**. Both names are suggestive of the great elevation of these lands. The Armenian Plateau sits at an average elevation of about 900 meters.

After the expulsion of the Armenians from the Armenian Plateau, Turkey began a systematic effort to remove Armenian *names* from the region, as well. Turkey changed Armenian Plateau to "Eastern Anatolia."

Historically, until the 1940s, the geographic region of Anatolia was recognized as extending west from the Aegean Sea and only as far east as the Armenian Plateau. The Mediterranean and Black Seas formed the south and north boundaries. Today, however, Turkey identifies all of Asiatic Turkey as Anatolia. By using this definition for Anatolia, the Armenian Plateau disappeared and became, instead, "*Eastern* Anatolia."

Identifying all of Asiatic Turkey as Anatolia is not accurate. The Armenian Plateau is not Eastern Anatolia. But Turkey's name change has been accepted by most of the world.

THE FORGOTTEN HOLY LAND

The Armenians are among the world's first Christians and they attribute their survival as a distinct people to their faith. Christianity united the nation during its long periods of foreign domination, and it enabled the Armenians to preserve their culture and national identity.

As Christians in a part of the world that would become, and which still is, predominantly Muslim, the Armenians were able to avoid assimilation and maintain a cohesive society even without political independence. They constructed religious shrines and stone monasteries that have survived nearly two millenia, and in doing so, the Armenians transformed their homeland into a Holy Land for Christendom.

These surviving shrines are today located in both the modern Republic of Armenia, and also in the historic Armenian homeland, which is located west of the republic in today's Turkey.

The earliest Christians in Armenia had been converted in the first century AD by Christ's apostles Thaddeus and Bartholomew. The missionary work of these Apostles eventually resulted in Armenia's official repudiation of paganism. In an acknowledgement of its ancient origins, the church of Armenia is called the Armenian Apostolic Church.

The nation officially adopted Christianity in AD 301 when a man named Gregory persuaded a king named Trdat that the king's realm should be Christian, and not pagan. The king, ironically, had imprisoned this man thirteen years earlier for the crime of preaching Christianity. Gregory had been sent to prison, actually a dungeon pit, for his supposed lunacy, and he survived only because other Christians had secretly brought him food and water.

The king didn't fare as well and had gone mad during Gregory's imprisonment. According to the legend, Gregory prayed for the king and cured him. And so the king expressed his gratitude by granting Gregory his freedom and by proclaiming Christianity as the official faith for the nation. Gregory was sainted, and he is now known as St. Gregory the Illuminator. He's the Illuminator because he illuminated Armenia with Christianity.

The pit where St. Gregory was imprisoned still exists, and a monastery was built above it as a demonstration of Christianity's triumph. Visitors can climb down into the pit, at the monastery of **Khor Virap**, in the town of Artashat, in today's Republic of Armenia.

Armenia's ancient Christian history is acknowledged in the names of its churches and monasteries. The ancient monasteries of **Soorp Bartholomew**, in the region of Van, and **Soorp Thaddeus**, located a short distance away, but in today's Republic of Iran, are named for the two apostles who had traveled to Armenia in the first century.

Soorp Bartholomew had been inaccessible for several decades because of its location in a restricted military zone in Turkey, near the border with Iran. In 2013 this restriction was lifted, and pilgrims may now view the ruins of this once majestic site.

And throughout Armenia, both Western and Eastern, and in regions as geographically diverse as Malatya, Palu, Ani, and Yerevan, there are countless churches and cathedrals named for St. Gregory.

Over the centuries, thousands of churches, monasteries, and Christian monuments were built throughout the part of Armenia that is today the Republic of Turkey. During the century since 1915, most of these sites have been destroyed or repurposed for other uses.

Despite this destruction, the lands of Armenia still have a wealth of ancient Christian sites. Too often, however, these sites are overlooked by religious pilgrims. As a result, Armenia has become the Forgotten Holy Land.

NEAR EAST RELIEF 100 YEARS AGO

In the spring of 1915, the massacres and deportations of the Armenian citizens of Ottoman Turkey began. When news of this holocaust reached the US, the American humanitarian organization Near East Relief rushed to help. This humanitarian effort was unprecedented in the US both for its magnitude and for its impassioned support.

Near East Relief was the first large scale international humanitarian relief effort of the US, and it is credited with raising $117 million in mostly-privately financed aid to the Armenians—an astonishing sum that, adjusted for inflation, is the equivalent of nearly $3 billion today.

From 1915 until 1930, when the relief efforts concluded, the organization saved the lives of 132,000 Armenian children who had become orphaned by the genocide. The organization also raised awareness of the genocide among Americans with its campaign to save the "starving Armenians."

The relief effort was launched following the urgent appeal of Henry Morgenthau, the US Ambassador to the Ottoman Empire, and it had the vocal support of US President Woodrow Wilson.

At first, assistance was administered through the US Embassy in Constantinople and through US missionaries. After the US entered the war against Turkey in 1917, this was no longer possible. Instead, relief was directed to regions outside Turkey where hundreds of thousands of Armenians had taken refuge.

Near East Relief played a critical role in the development of philanthropy in America. Its campaign to provide relief to the Armenians gave the US an international voice in humanitarian affairs. Their efforts also helped the Armenian nation survive.

Armenian Deportees, 1915
Photo by Armin T Wegner, Courtesy of the Armenian National Institute

ARMENIANS IN THE WORLD, 1914

The worldwide population of Armenians in 1914 was divided almost evenly between Western Armenia in the Ottoman Empire, and Eastern Armenia in the Russian Empire. The Diaspora accounted for less than 10 percent of the Armenians at this time.

Courtesy of Robert H. Hewsen

KUBAN
22,000

TEREK
23,000

SUKHUM
18,000

KUTAIS
8,000

RUSSIAN EMPIRE

TIFLIS
395,000

DAGESTAN
5,000

CASPIAN SEA

BATUM
21,000

ZAKATALI
3,000

BLACK SEA

KASTOMONU
10,000

ELIZAVETPOL
397,000

BAKU
114,000

TRABZON
65,000

KARS
114,000

YEREVAN
598,000

L. Sevan

SEBASTIA (Sivas)
225,000

ANKARA
115,000

ERZERUM
215,000

OTTOMAN EMPIRE

KHARPERT
(Mamuret-Ülaziz)
204,000

BITLIS
198,000

L. Van

PERSIAN EMPIRE
140,000

KONYA
25,000

DIYARBAKIR
124,000

VAN
197,000

ADANA
118,000

HALEP
186,000

ZOR

MOSUL 800

MEDITERRANEAN SEA

8.7%
Elsewhere

Russian Empire
45.9%

Total
4,470,000
Armenians

45.4%
Ottoman
Empire

Armenian Population

	600,000
	300,000
	200,000
	100,000
	10,000
	1,000

ARMENIANS IN THE WORLD, 1926

The population of Armenians in their Western Armenia homeland had been almost completely eradicated by 1926. Seventy-five percent of the Armenians were killed. The survivors fled the region and helped to create a flourishing Diaspora that now covers the entire world.

Courtesy of Robert H. Hewsen

KARACHAI-CHERKESIA
9,800

KABARDIA
19,200

CHECHNYA
21,400

U N I O N   Of

N. OSSETIA
400

ABKHAZIA
25,700

DAGESTAN
5,900

CASPIAN SEA

S O V I E T

S. OSSETIA
1,400

ADJARIA
10,500

GEORGIAN S.S.R.
269,500

S O C I A L I S T

KASTOMONU
3,400

BLACK SEA

R E P U B L I C S

TRABZON
300

ARMENIAN
S. S. R.

743,600

Nagorno Karabakh
Autonomous Region
(ARTSAKH)

AZER. S.S.R.
159,000

L. Sevan

SEBASTIA (Sivas)
5,100

ERZERUM
0

111,700

R E P U B L I C

ANKARA
8,500

KHARPERT
(Mamuret-Ülaziz)
5,000

NAKHICHEVAN
11,300

130,000

PERSIAN EMPIRE
(IRAN)

of

BITLIS
0

L. Van

KONYA
800

T U R K E Y

VAN
0

Armenian Population

4.3%
Turkey

DIYARBAKIR
500

Total
2,900,000
Armenians

USSR
54.1%

750,000
300,000
200,000
100,000
10,000
1,000

ADANA
0

URFA
0

41.6%
Elsewhere

8,500

HATAY

S Y R I A   120,000

I R A Q

MEDITERRANEAN SEA

ONE HUNDRED YEARS IN DENIAL

One hundred years ago, the Turkish Ottoman Empire lashed out at what Turkish leaders today say was a threat to its survival.

Under the cover of World War I, the Empire initiated a campaign to eradicate its Christian Armenian minority, a national group that had lived on the Armenian Plateau of Asia Minor—the historic Armenian homeland—without interruption for 3,000 years. In doing so, the Ottomans committed the first genocide of the modern era.

Most historians today reject the claim that the Christian Armenians were a threat to the survival of the vast Ottoman Empire. Instead, the so-called threat was a creation of Turkish propaganda to rationalize its wartime atrocities against its Armenian subjects.

Genocide scholars such as Vahakn Dadrian, Ph D, today recognize the genocide as having been conceived as a radical solution to a lingering conflict with the Armenians. World War I merely gave the Ottoman Turks the long sought opportunity to solve the "Armenian Question" once, and for all.

Throughout the 1800s, concurrent with the rise of the modern nation-state, there was a shaping of national consciousness among the Armenians of historic Armenia. The Armenians experienced a national awakening after centuries of submission to Ottoman rule. The West encouraged this awakening. In the process, some scholars contend that the Western powers created an "Armenian Question" by creating aspirations for cultural autonomy among Turkey's Armenian community.

Other leading historians, however, point to the inherent inequities of Ottoman society as the progenitor of the conflict with the Armenians. The Islamic tenets and dogmas of Ottoman theocracy created and fostered inequities, prejudices, and a system of discrimination that rendered the Empire pregnant with conflict involving the non-Islamic nationalities, of whom the Armenians were one such group.

Armenian Deportees, 1915
Photo Courtesy of the Library of Congress

By the 1880s and 1890s, the insular society of Armenians was also becoming increasingly exposed to Western ideology through the presence of missionaries, business people, and foreign diplomats. Europeans insisted that Ottomans reform their ways, and treat their Christian Armenian subjects less oppressively.

Young Armenians who had studied in Europe and then returned to the Empire with Western ideals also became proponents of socio-political change. The Ottomans responded to all of this with increasing discrimination and retribution against the Armenians.

By the end of the nineteenth century, the Ottoman Empire was in decay, and its leadership felt threatened, this time from within—from the Armenians who lived in the heartland of Asia Minor, the Armenian Plateau, which was the mainland of the Ottoman Empire. There could be no compromises.

A series of massacres began in 1894. In the region of Sasun, Kurdish tribes who had been organized by the Turks into official irregular armed units attacked an Armenian village. Turkish officials responded with troops, but they arrested only Armenians. The Kurds had been, in effect, deputized by the Ottomans to keep the Armenians in line. This massacre was the first of many that would visit the Armenians throughout the 1890s.

This policy of massacre was a means of maintaining the decaying status quo as the preferred alternative to reform and concessions to the Armenians. One noted historian calls the massacres a "diplomatic note" issued by the Turks to the intermeddling West. By the time the episodes had all concluded, 300,000 Armenians had been killed.

At the close of the 1800s and into the early years of the 1900s, there was also a great political upheaval throughout the Ottoman Empire. Through wars of independence, the Turks lost control of their subjects in the Balkans and the Middle East. Their empire was shrinking. An Armenian reform movement, meanwhile, was seeking to restructure Ottoman society based on the Western ideal of equality of all citizens before the law.

For a brief moment, Armenians held out hope for better conditions. Some of them hoped for independence, too, although the clergy, and especially the wealthy Armenians of western Anatolia, generally preferred to remain submissive to Turkish rule. The Young Turks seized power in 1908, bringing with them the false promise of reform.

The promise faded fast, and in the Mediterranean coast town of Adana, a frenzy of violence resulted in the deaths of 30,000 Armenians. Thousands of Armenians were burnt alive in their homes, schools and hospitals. Press reports in the New York *Times* called the event a "holocaust."

The killings were meant to frighten the Armenians and so dampen their expectations. Historians generally refer to these events, from roughly 1894 through 1909, as "massacres," and not as "genocide." The crimes were committed in isolated and distinct pockets of the Ottoman Empire, and many characterize the violence as *ad hoc*, and as instigated largely by Kurdish tribes acting under the color of Turkish authority.

By 1914, these *ad hoc* killings would mutate into what the noted British historian Jay Winter has characterized as "total war" upon the Armenians. Total war provided the space in which genocidal crimes could take place with impunity, and it was during the First World War that the Turkish and Kurdish populations showed their propensity to mobilize themselves.

There was a cultivation of hatred, and the incentive for violence was raised through the proclamation of an Islamic "Holy War" (*Jihad*). The Armenians were vilified, as were the Jews in Nazi Germany 20 years leter.

The morbid efficiency of the genocide is evident from the statistics. Before 1915, the Armenian population in historic Armenia numbered roughly 2 million. By 1923, there were roughly 100,000 Armenians remaining, almost entirely in the western Anatolian city of Istanbul. The historic homeland of the Armenians had been completely emptied of its indigenous population. The Turks established in its place the modern Republic of Turkey that, by 1923, had gained international recognition.

The founding fathers of the modern Republic of Turkey participated in the genocide. From 1920 to 1923, insurgent Kemalists fulfilled their goal of the establishment of a modern Turkey partly through the ethnic cleansing of whatever remained of the surviving indigenous Armenian population of Asiatic Turkey.

Tens of thousands of Armenian survivors of the genocide were killed or expelled as part of this operation. This operation pursued survivors who had fled the Empire, as well, by attacking Armenian refugees in parts of Armenia that were controlled by Russia, in towns such as Alexandropol (today's Gyumri). The genocide was thus international in scope, and the modern Republic of Turkey was complicit in its conduct.

Between 400,000 and 500,000 Armenians survived the deportations, and settled as refugees, mainly in the Middle East, Europe, the US and the Soviet Union. The remaining Armenian population of about 1.5 million had perished. To have been an Armenian in 1923 meant that you were either dead or a refugee.

Turkish revisionists claim, among other things, that there is no proof that 1.5 million Armenians died. It would seem, instead, that they simply vanished.

Alternately, Turkish apologists state that many Armenians died, but there is no proof that the Turks intended them to die. It seems improbable, however, that more than one million could have perished, throughout all regions of the Empire, by accident. One may instead infer intent from such widespread destruction.

Still other defenders of the Turkish record insist that the Armenians "perished" because they were subversive and a threat to Turkey's survival. In essence, the claim is that there was no genocide of the Armenians, and besides, they got what they deserved.

The matter of intent of genocide, or to use the terminology that was current at the time, the intent of "centrally organized and comprehensive mass murder," was documented thoroughly at the time, however. United States Consul Leslie Davis, serving in Kharpert, was a witness to the atrocities, and he filed reports on the matter to the US Dept. of State. He wrote in 1917 that the killings had transformed Kharpert into a Slaughterhouse Province.

Evidence was presented at Turkish courts-martial in 1919 and 1920. Similar documentary evidence was produced by Turkey's allies. More than a dozen ambassadors, consuls, vice-consuls and officials flooded Berlin and Vienna with first-hand testimonies about the genocidal intent of the wartime deportations of the Armenians.

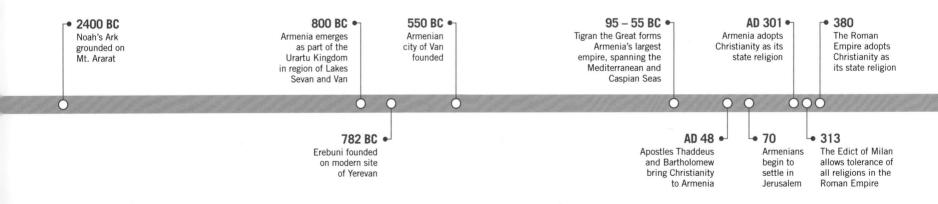

2400 BC
Noah's Ark grounded on Mt. Ararat

800 BC
Armenia emerges as part of the Urartu Kingdom in region of Lakes Sevan and Van

550 BC
Armenian city of Van founded

95 – 55 BC
Tigran the Great forms Armenia's largest empire, spanning the Mediterranean and Caspian Seas

AD 301
Armenia adopts Christianity as its state religion

380
The Roman Empire adopts Christianity as its state religion

782 BC
Erebuni founded on modern site of Yerevan

AD 48
Apostles Thaddeus and Bartholomew bring Christianity to Armenia

70
Armenians begin to settle in Jerusalem

313
The Edict of Milan allows tolerance of all religions in the Roman Empire

The massacres aroused indignation from the West. The US instituted a massive relief effort and delivered $117 million in assistance to the surviving refugees, but the killings were soon forgotten.

There are today only about 60,000 Armenians remaining in Turkey, almost all of them in Istanbul, which is Turkey's only major city in Europe. Armenians who survived, or who returned to the eastern provinces of Turkey are today known as the hidden Armenians, because they must hide their ethnicity in order to avoid persecution.

Turkey denies that the events of 1915-1923 constituted genocide. In 2014, during the run-up to the centennary of the start of the genocide, the Turkish Prime Minister offered his condolences to the grandchildren of those who were killed, but he stopped short of admitting guilt.

One hundred years after the start of the genocide, Armenians and Turks have no diplomatic relations, a closed border, and scant prospects for putting the past behind them. The genocide that was begun on April 24, 1915 has not ended but is instead merely in its final stage: denial.

BY THE END OF **WORLD WAR I,** MORE THAN **150,000** CHILDREN HAD BECOME **ORPHANED** BY THE **GENOCIDE**

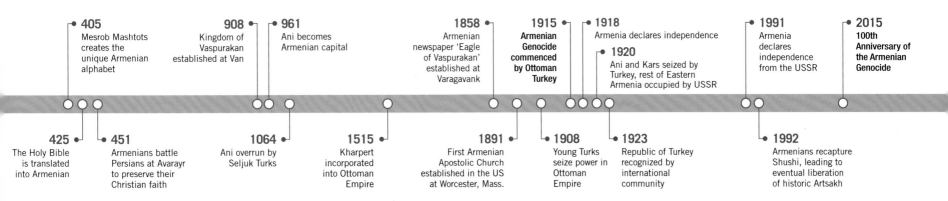

405
Mesrob Mashtots creates the unique Armenian alphabet

908
Kingdom of Vaspurakan established at Van

961
Ani becomes Armenian capital

1858
Armenian newspaper 'Eagle of Vaspurakan' established at Varagavank

1915
Armenian Genocide commenced by Ottoman Turkey

1918
Armenia declares independence

1920
Ani and Kars seized by Turkey, rest of Eastern Armenia occupied by USSR

1991
Armenia declares independence from the USSR

2015
100th Anniversary of the Armenian Genocide

425
The Holy Bible is translated into Armenian

451
Armenians battle Persians at Avarayr to preserve their Christian faith

1064
Ani overrun by Seljuk Turks

1515
Kharpert incorporated into Ottoman Empire

1891
First Armenian Apostolic Church established in the US at Worcester, Mass.

1908
Young Turks seize power in Ottoman Empire

1923
Republic of Turkey recognized by international community

1992
Armenians recapture Shushi, leading to eventual liberation of historic Artsakh

THE DEPORTATION AND MASSACRE OF THE ARMENIAN NATION, 1915-1923

On the eve of World War I, there were two million Armenians in the Ottoman Empire. By 1923, seventy-five percent had been killed in the first systematic genocide of modern times. This map illustrates where and how the nation perished. On April 24, 1915, the intellectuals and leaders of the Armenian nation living in Constantinople were arrested and deported eastward to Anatolia. The blue crosses mark the locations of their subsequent execution. The red dots illustrate the relative numbers of Armenians who were killed throughout the Ottoman Empire. The arrows show the so-called "deportation routes" for the women and children who were expelled from their homes after the men had been killed.

Courtesy of Robert H. Hewsen

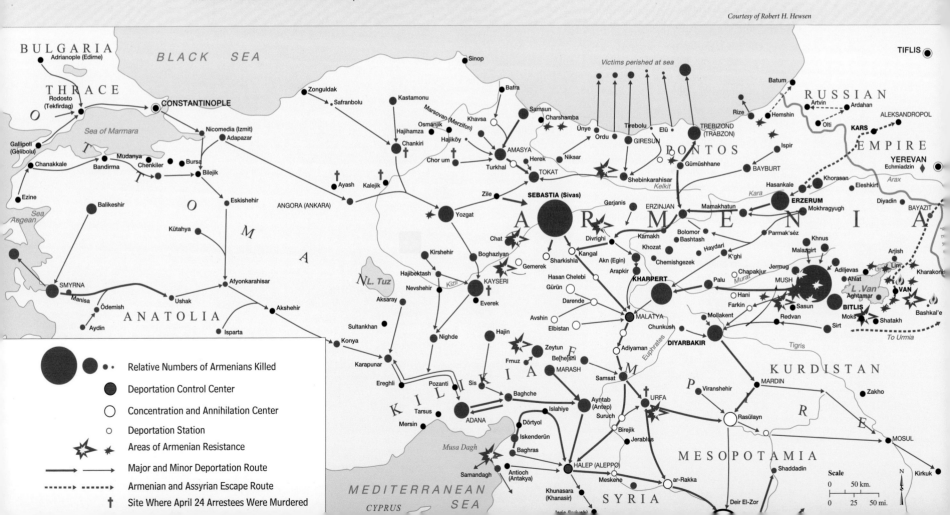

Legend:

- Relative Numbers of Armenians Killed
- Deportation Control Center
- Concentration and Annihilation Center
- Deportation Station
- Areas of Armenian Resistance
- Major and Minor Deportation Route
- Armenian and Assyrian Escape Route
- † Site Where April 24 Arrestees Were Murdered

HRANT DINK

Hrant Dink was one of the most prominent Armenian voices in Turkey at the time of his death in 2007. He had dedicated his life to fighting racism and supporting freedom of expression.

Dink became an enduring international symbol of these struggles after he was murdered. To many Armenians, he also became a symbol of the continued genocide of the Armenian people.

For the decade prior to his death, Dink had been the editor of *Agos*, a weekly Armenian newspaper that he published in Istanbul. His columns regularly addressed what he saw as the institutionalized racism against Armenians and other minorities in Turkey. He did not shy away from characterizing the mass killings of the Armenians in 1915 as genocide.

Because of the content of his writings and speeches, Dink was prosecuted and convicted for "denigrating Turkishness" in violation of Article 301 of Turkey's penal code. The high-profile criminal charges contributed to an atmosphere of vilification of Dink. This atmosphere led, ultimately, to Dink's murder.

Ironically, Dink had been working to reconcile Armenians and Turks at the time of his murder. In an interview with the Committee to Protect Journalists two years before his death, Dink is quoted saying "I want to write and ask how we can change this historical conflict into peace."

The stories that Dink published in *Agos* were written in both Armenian and Turkish, which he said was in furtherance of his attempt to bridge the gap between the Turkish and Armenian communities and to help create a dialogue between them. Dink did bridge some gaps and he did start a dialogue. But his columns and his televised commentaries, spoken in fluent Turkish, also antagonized some opponents.

Shortly after 3 o'clock on a Friday afternoon in September, Dink had just concluded an appointment and was returning to his office in Istanbul. The street was crowded with pedestrians. One of those pedestrians was Dink's assassin, a man who police would later identify as a Turkish nationalist.

The assassin waited until Dink was right outside the front door of his office building and then approached Dink from behind. He fired three shots at the back of Dink's head from point blank range.

A memorial plaque today marks the spot on the sidewalk where Dink's life was ended. He had been born 53 years earlier in Malatya, and was the descendant of survivors of the Armenian holocaust. He was also its latest victim.

Ani, the city of 1,001 churches

Ani and Kars

Kars

Rep. Armenia

Artsakh

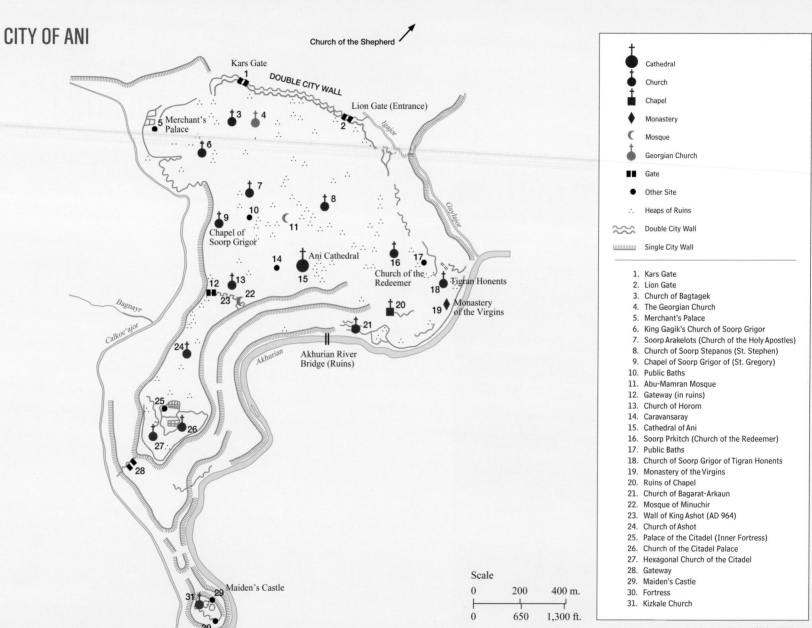

CITY OF ANI

Church of the Shepherd

Kars Gate

DOUBLE CITY WALL

Lion Gate (Entrance)

Igajor

5 Merchant's Palace

†3 †4

2

†6

Gavlajor

†7

†8

†9 10

11

Chapel of Soorp Grigor

14

Ani Cathedral

16 17

15

Church of the Redeemer

18 †Tigran Honents

12 †13

22

23

20

19 ◆ Monastery of the Virgins

21

Bagnayr

Calkoc'ajor

24†

Akhurian

Akhurian River Bridge (Ruins)

25

26

27

28

Maiden's Castle

31 29

30

Legend

✚	Cathedral
✚	Church
■	Chapel
◆	Monastery
☽	Mosque
●	Georgian Church
■■	Gate
●	Other Site
∴	Heaps of Ruins
〜	Double City Wall
⊔⊔⊔	Single City Wall

1. Kars Gate
2. Lion Gate
3. Church of Bagtagek
4. The Georgian Church
5. Merchant's Palace
6. King Gagik's Church of Soorp Grigor
7. Soorp Arakelots (Church of the Holy Apostles)
8. Church of Soorp Stepanos (St. Stephen)
9. Chapel of Soorp Grigor of (St. Gregory)
10. Public Baths
11. Abu-Mamran Mosque
12. Gateway (in ruins)
13. Church of Horom
14. Caravansaray
15. Cathedral of Ani
16. Soorp Prkitch (Church of the Redeemer)
17. Public Baths
18. Church of Soorp Grigor of Tigran Honents
19. Monastery of the Virgins
20. Ruins of Chapel
21. Church of Bagarat-Arkaun
22. Mosque of Minuchir
23. Wall of King Ashot (AD 964)
24. Church of Ashot
25. Palace of the Citadel (Inner Fortress)
26. Church of the Citadel Palace
27. Hexagonal Church of the Citadel
28. Gateway
29. Maiden's Castle
30. Fortress
31. Kizkale Church

Scale

0   200   400 m.

0   650   1,300 ft.

Courtesy of Robert H. Hewsen

Ani

INTRODUCTION

Ani is the fabled city of a thousand churches and the capital of a once-mighty Armenian kingdom. The city flourished during an Armenian silver age that lasted for about a century beginning in AD 961.

For the past three hundred fifty years, however, the city has been largely abandoned, and it has been completely uninhabited for the past century. Many people today call Ani a ghost town. For Armenians, however, the city is alive. There is no place else in the world with a greater concentration of Armenian churches and artifacts than within the walls of Ani.

The remains of the city's massive walls, stately arches, and carved domes "testify to the audacity of the people who built this place," wrote the New York *Times* in a cover travel story that was published shortly after Turkey first eased its ban on travel to Ani. The *Times* celebrated Ani, without equivocation, as an Armenian capital, and noted that "stone churches are covered with inscriptions that are clearly legible to anyone who can read Armenian."

Ani sits directly on the current border between Armenia and Turkey and is located within the region of Kars on the Armenian Plateau. The shallow Akhurian River keeps this part of historic Armenia separate and apart from the current Republic of Armenia.

Ani's rise to wealth and glory began in AD 961 when the royal Bagratuni family of Armenia chose Ani as its capital. The city quickly grew to have a population of about 100,000 people and,

supposedly, more than one thousand churches. The ancient historian **Matteos Urhayatsi (Matthew of Edessa)**, long ago wrote that Ani was home to one-thousand-and-one churches. Ever since, Ani and the number 1,001 have been irrevocably linked in our minds.

It is unlikely that there were ever really 1,001 churches at Ani. Still, the actual number must have been substantial—and close enough to the truth that the number has persisted in our consciousness for a millennium.

A traveler to Ani in the seventeenth century reported the presence of 200 churches. Even this lower number, tallied at a time when Ani was enduring its final decline, would substantiate the capital's claim to be Armenia's city of churches.

The modern history of Ani has been heartbreaking.

At the end of the nineteenth century, Ani and the surrounding region of Kars were within the Russian Empire. A Russian archaeologist recognized the historic value of the site, and he began excavations at Ani in 1892. After more than two decades of work, he had stored thousands of artifacts at a museum he had opened within the city's walls.

Many of these artifacts were looted or destroyed when Turkey captured the site from Armenia in 1918.

Armenia couldn't recover the lost artifacts, but it was able to reassert its control over Ani. When the independent Republic of

Armenia was established later in 1918, Ani and the surrounding region of Kars were both included within Armenia's borders.

The Republic of Armenia's control of Ani and Kars lasted just about two years.

Turkey invaded Armenia in 1920, seized Ani and Kars, and incorporated them both into the newly formed Republic of Turkey. The same year, Armenia was overrun by the Soviet Union. The USSR in 1921 signed a treaty with Turkey officially ceding to them Ani and Kars. Armenia wasn't consulted.

One of Turkey's first acts of sovereignty over Ani, in 1921, was to order that the monuments of the city be eradicated.

This obscene order was not completely fulfilled, but many Armenian churches and monuments in Ani were nevertheless destroyed. Graves were plundered. And the evidence of the Russian excavations that had begun in 1892 was obliterated.

During the decades that followed, an effort was made through diplomacy to reestablish Armenian sovereignty over the limited area of the old city of Ani, for reasons of culture and historic preservation. These efforts were rebuffed.

A proposal to open a border crossing so that Armenians could visit Ani directly from Armenia was also rejected. Present-day Turkey retains control over this ancient Armenian capital.

For most of the past century, Turkey has characterized the region of Ani, which sits directly on the modern border of Turkey and Armenia, as a military zone. Tourists needed a special permit to enter the region and they had to travel to a military office in Kars, at a distance of about 45 kilometers, in order to get it. This red tape discouraged visitors generally, and visitors with Armenian surnames, particularly, from visiting Ani.

Photography was strictly prohibited. Uniformed soldiers patrolled the site to ensure there were no violations of this rule.

Today, however, the military designation has been lifted, and tourism at Ani is encouraged. Photography is permitted. The sight of a tour bus in the parking lot outside Ani is no longer remarkable.

During the past several years, the Turkish authorities have even rebuilt some structures at Ani. Some have said that their motivation for this reconstruction is political. The architectural methods used in the so-called "restoration" of Armenian churches have also been criticized, with justification.

Apart from the criticism, however, the opening of Ani, and the attention that has been given to rebuilding some of the ruins, suggests that the current custodians of this area see Ani as a site that is now worth saving and showcasing. That 1921 government order to destroy the place has apparently been repudiated.

For the first time in a century, pilgrims can freely visit what's left of the Armenian capital of Ani. The site is still uninhabited, but the privilege of full access has made it possible for us to imagine an Ani that is once again thriving and vibrant.

The Ancient People of Ani

The name **Ani** is believed to have been derived from an ancient race of people who once lived in Armenia.

According to the first century Greek geographer Strabo, a people who were known as either the *Aniani* or the *Aenia* had lived in the area of Shirak, which is the region of the Armenian Plateau that became home to Ani.

At the time that Ani first acquired its name, the area appears to have been a small village of no great significance. Ani's modest beginning stands in contrast to its later status during the tenth century as a glorious Armenian city of many churches that rivaled the capitals of Europe in culture and wealth and splendor.

The Chapel of Soorp Grigor (St. Gregory)

HIGHLIGHTS OF ANI AND KARS

The **Cathedral of Ani** is perhaps the single most recognizable monument within the city walls of Ani. This massive structure dwarfs every other building within the city. Because of its prominent location, this is also the first building that most visitors to Ani will view.

Most of the cathedral's drum, as well as its dome, have collapsed. The gaping hole resulting in the roof has shed light on what would otherwise be a dark and mystical interior. Other sections of the building are today at risk of collapse, and there has been an attempt in recent years to shore-up the structure and to make some structural repairs.

The Cathedral was constructed in AD 1010 and is known to Armenians as **Soorp Astvatsatsin**, or the **Church of the Holy Mother of God**. The majestic architecture of this building has been imitated, most notably by the designs of the cathedrals in the towns of Talin and Gyumri, which are both located in today's Armenia.

The ruins of Armenian churches, as well as of some historically significant non-Armenian structures, fill the now-uninhabited city, and viewing them all will take at least one-half day of walking.

The **Church of the Holy Redeemer**, also known as the **Church of the Holy Savior**, which dates back to AD 1035, offers a dramatic sight. The thousand-year-old structure was split in two during a thunderstorm one half century ago, and now stands like an egg that has been cracked open.

Outside the walls of Ani, the cave dwellings that once constituted the suburbs of the city are still present and can be freely viewed by visitors. The walls of the city themselves, in various states of repair and ruin, are remarkable, and are worth studying.

Every visit to Ani usually includes a visit to Kars. This is because Ani is uninhabited, and has no lodging. Kars, which is located about 45 kilometers away, is the nearest city with hotels.

Logistics aside, Kars is worth visiting in its own right. Kars is home to the **Kars Castle**, the **Church of the Holy Apostles**, and the ruins of the home of Armenian poet **Yeghishe Charents**.

The Church of the Holy Apostles is outfitted today as a mosque, but the engravings of the twelve apostles that adorn its drum, and from which the church takes its name, are still present. The Armenian name for this stately church is **Soorp Arakelots**.

The role of Kars in Armenian history is as storied as the role of Ani. Indeed, its contribution to *modern* Armenian history is more significant. Kars was a part of the modern Republic of Armenia until 1920, and had a large Armenian population. The region figured prominently in the struggle of the Armenian nation to survive during the closing years of World War I.

Outside the city, and throughout the region of Kars, the ruins of numerous Armenian sites are still present and can be visited without great difficulty, although hiking is required in each instance.

Horomos, also known as **Goshavank** or **Koshavank**, is located 15 kilometers north of Ani. Horomos has not fared well during the past 100 years. This thousand-year old monastery survived intact for 900 years, until 1920 when Turkey seized the region of Kars from Armenia. Today the site is in ruins and may soon be a complete loss.

Mren is south of Ani, on the border across from the town of Anipemza in today's Armenia. Mren was also seized by Turkey in 1920, and is today also in great peril. **Khtzkonk Monastery**, which is known locally by its Turkish name **Besh Kilise (Five Churches)**, is also south of Ani, and demands to be seen. The name Besh Kilise has persisted, even though the Turkish Army has blown up four of the churches and only one now remains.

These sites make the entire region of Kars, and not just Ani, a recommended destination for the pilgrim seeking the sights of historic Armenia.

A BRIEF HISTORY OF ANI

The ascension of Ani as an Armenian center of culture and commerce began in AD 961 with the decision of the Bagratuni Dynasty to relocate the capital of its Armenian kingdom here.

Thus began a silver age for the Armenians during which numerous monasteries, churches, and public buildings were erected throughout the lands. Armenian culture flourished, and the Armenians themselves prospered.

Ashot Bagratuni had established his Armenian kingdom in AD 884, and the royal family had briefly chosen the towns of Bagaran, and then nearby Kars, as their capitals. They finally settled upon Ani in AD 961, and immediately began construction of major building projects.

Through their construction, the royal family transformed Ani from a simple fortress to a thriving capital.

Their priority upon settling Ani appears to have been defense. Within three years, by AD 964, the kingdom had erected the first of the capital's two fortified protective walls under the leadership of King Ashot III. The second wall was completed in AD 978 by King Smbat II. The walls included towers and gates, and the structure is largely still standing today.

These walls did not completely encircle Ani. This wasn't necessary. The geography of Ani provided most of the city's defense. This is because Ani is sited on a triangular bluff of land, with rivers looping around three sides, from east to south to west. Only the north side, the side with the double walls, was naturally weak. For added measure, the double walls that were built here were fronted by a moat, as well.

The most prominent and historically important buildings of Ani—buildings whose ruins survive to this day—appear to have been constructed in the century following the completion of the defensive walls.

The Akhurian River marks the boundary between today's Armenia and Ani

The Monastery of the Virgins

Under the leadership of the Bagratuni dynasty, the Armenian kingdom at Ani became a great power. The kingdom fielded an army of 80,000 soldiers, and the city of Ani alone had a population of about 100,000. The scholar of Armenian history Robert H. Hewsen characterizes Ani at its zenith as a large urban complex, "much larger than any contemporary city in Western Europe."

Ani's commerce with other kingdoms and principalities expanded and Ani became prosperous. According to Hewsen, Ani's trade grew "until it was said in the East that no caravan was on the road but for its sake." The prosperity and security of Armenian Ani lasted for a bit more than one century.

The last Armenian king of Ani, King Gagik II, was compelled in AD 1045 to cede the kingdom to the Byzantines. The rule of the Byzantines was inept and brief. They lost Ani to an invasion of Seljuk Turks after just twenty years, in 1064. Another Bagratuni kingdom, located at Kars, fell the following year, in 1065.

The destruction of Ani by the Seljuk Turks in 1064 did not signal the end of Ani. To the contrary, Ani continued to survive for at least another three hundred years, under a variety of rulers, passing from Muslims to Georgians to Mongols, and for brief periods, to Armenians.

By the fourteenth century, according to the scholar of Armenian history Richard G. Hovannisian, the combined forces of Tamerlane's pillaging armies and powerful earthquakes had humbled the once proud capital.

Hovannisian describes the slow and deliberate demise of Ani that began in 1319, following a devastating earthquake, and which continued for centuries: "The structural integrity of the grand palaces and churches gradually succumbed to the forces of nature. [T]he local Turkish and Kurdish inhabitants turned the land into pastoral grazing grounds, plundered the graves and storehouses, and carried away the large stones to build their own houses, stables, and fences."

Historians disagree about the role of the earthquake of 1319 in the demise of Ani. The earthquake that is recorded in that year occurred far away, in today's Iran. And there is no evidence of massive destruction in Ani at that time. Ani appears to have been spared.

Instead, some scholars contend that Ani was already in decline in the fourteenth century, and that the appearance in 1394 of the warrior Tamerlane sealed Ani's fate. The city staggered on for another two hundred years after Tamerlane's invasion, but never regained its previous grandeur.

Ani was incorporated into the Ottoman Empire in 1579. A town with a small population persisted within Ani's walls until the middle of the 1600s but by the end of the 1600s Ani had become abandoned by all—except for a tiny stewardship of Armenian monks who may have persisted until as late as 1895, or even a bit later.

The Russian Empire took control of Ani after its successful war with Ottoman Turkey in 1878, and the city appears to have been rediscovered not by settlers, but by Russian and European travelers, during the years immediately before and after this conquest.

A Russian archaeologist rediscovered Ani in the late 1800s, and conducted significant excavations over the course of two decades.

The most widely heralded account of a modern European visitor to Ani is the account by **H. F. B. Lynch**. The traveler Lynch wrote that during his visit to Ani in 1893, "an old priest with a few attendants were the sole inhabitants—they and the owls."

Within a few short years, even this Armenian priest would be gone.

Ani, emptied of its people, was briefly restored to Armenia in 1918. Two years later, in 1920, the city was taken by Turkey, which has held Ani ever since.

Ani at the End of the Nineteenth Century

The British adventurist H. F. B. Lynch traveled throughout the Turkish and Russian provinces of Armenia in 1893-94 and again in 1898. He published his observations in 1901 in the two-volume tome *Armenia: Travels and Studies*.

Lynch describes his arrival on horseback at Ani: "It was late afternoon when we reached the walls of the ancient capital and passed within the gateway. No massive doors creaked upon their hinges; we rode through empty archways into a deserted town.

"From among the debris of the public and private buildings rose the well-preserved remains of a number of handsome edifices—here an elegant church, there a polygonal chapel. An old priest with a few attendants were the sole inhabitants—they and the owls.

"We had only to follow the track to be brought to the humble tenement in which the priest lived. He stepped forth to meet us, a grey head, a feeble figure; he walked with difficulty, and with the demeanor of a man who is awaiting death.

"He told us that he had dwelt here since 1880, the only custodian of these priceless architectural treasures, and the only exponent of the topography of the site. He had been attacked in his house by a band of Kurds in 1886; they had inflicted knife wounds, and stripped him of everything he possessed.

"We remained two whole days within the walls of Ani, examining the creations of a vanished civilization, and collecting material."

Archaeological Excavations

The first excavations at Ani, and the most significant, were carried out in 1892 and 1893 under the direction of the Russian archaeologist **Nikolai (Nicholas) Marr**.

Marr worked with the St. Petersburg Academy of Sciences, and he followed up with further excavations and studies from 1904 to 1917. His work unearthed priceless artifacts as he reached down, layer upon layer, into the history of ancient Ani.

Marr's work has contributed to our understanding of the physical appearance of Ani. The city was densely populated, and densely built, as well. Within the perimeter of Ani, bounded by its walls and two deep ravines, there was no open space. Buildings covered the entirety of Ani.

Today, the debris of the buildings that once occupied Ani gives the city a rubble-strewn appearance. The "broader portion of the site," writes H. F. B. Lynch, "is covered with the debris of private dwellings, not one of which has remained erect. They must have been packed together in a most uncomfortable manner, and they were probably built for the greater part of inferior material." The well-constructed churches, by contrast, have fared better.

The Armenian history scholar Richard G. Hovannisian wrote about Marr's work in a passage that appears in Hovannisian's *Armenian Kars and Ani*: "Marr and his colleagues had grand designs for reviving Ani—restoring the cathedral, creating parks, and opening a school to educate the local Armenian children—but these plans were cut short by the turmoil of 1914-1921: World War I, the Russian revolutions, and the Turkish invasions."

One can only imagine the history that might have been preserved here, and throughout Armenia, if the turmoil of 1914-1921 could have been averted.

Still, Marr was able to make detailed studies of many of the churches and buildings of Ani, and he outfitted a pair of museums within the city walls, which he filled with the treasures he had excavated.

A photographer named **Aram Vrouyr** accompanied Marr and created a photographic record of many of the sites during these years, as well. **Artashes Vrouyr**, the son of Aram, worked as his father's assistant. Decades later this dutiful son wrote the memoir "Anioom," which provides an account of their activities as the photographers of Ani. The English language translation of Anioom is "At Ani."

Much of what had been excavated and cataloged by Marr was destroyed during Turkey's two invasions of Ani and Kars in 1918 and in 1920. The two museums were looted. The destruction has made the photographs of Aram and Artashes Vrouyr a priceless record of Ani's condition just prior to 1915.

The website of the **Virtual Ani** project contains a detailed report about Marr's excavations, and explains what happened to the cultural treasures of Ani during the impending invasion by Turkey.

In 1918, with Ani under threat of invasion by the Turkish army, one of the archaeologists who had been working with Marr attempted to carry the treasures to safety. This man, Ashkharbek Kalantar, was able to remove some artifacts to Yerevan. The items that he saved are now on display at the National Museum of History. But many artifacts were left behind, especially the bulky carved stones, which were too heavy to move.

The Virtual Ani project reports that Kalantar managed to make a final visit to Ani in 1922. He "found that the main museum and the stonework museum [containing the artifacts that they had uncovered] had been looted and destroyed, their doors and windows wrenched off, and their roofs removed."

Marr apparently was already aware of the destruction by this time. He had published an essay the previous year, in 1921, pointing out the irony that the people who had destroyed the museums were probably the same Muslim villagers that he had employed as workers during excavations.

The World's Eyes on Ani

The city of Ani in 2012 was placed on a "tentative list" for inclusion as a World Heritage site by the **United Nations Educational, Scientific and Cultural Organization (UNESCO)**. According to the UNESCO statement about the listing, "Ani has a special place in the history of medieval art and history."

The inclusion of Ani on this tentative UNESCO list was made upon the application of Turkey. A cultural site may be considered for addition to the UNESCO World Heritage list only upon the nomination of the government of the state in which the site is located.

If Ani gains a place on the World Heritage list, it will be the first Armenian site in Turkey with this designation, although Turkey may not agree with this claim. The reason? Turkey considers Ani to be a multi-ethnic and multi-cultural site, and does not attribute Ani's cultural or historic status to the Armenians. Turkey's nomination of Ani, which is reported on the website of UNESCO, is ambiguous about any Armenian connection to the city.

The **World Monuments Fund (WMF)**, a private non-governmental organization, identified the Ani Cathedral and Ani's Church of the Redeemer (Soorp Prkitch) in 1996 as two of the world's "at risk" sites of significant cultural heritage. This organization clearly identifies both sites as Armenian. The WMF has been collaborating since 2011 with the Turkish authorities to conserve these two sites.

The Armenian Cathedral of Mren, which is located south of Ani, was added in 2014 to the World Monuments Funds' list of "at risk" cultural sites in Turkey.

The **Global Heritage Fund**, a non-profit organization that operates from Palo Alto, California, identified Ani in 2010 as one of 12 ancient landmarks worldwide that are on the verge of vanishing.

This organization is unambiguous about Ani's status as an Armenian capital. The organization describes Ani as "settled by Armenians in the tenth and eleventh centuries," and reports that Ani holds churches and other buildings that helped inspire the Gothic style across Europe. Ani is today at risk, says the organization, because of insufficient management, and because of looting and vandalism.

Ani on the Web

The website of the **Virtual Ani** project is operated by experts on Armenian architecture. The site includes news and articles about the condition of ancient Armenian sites throughout historic Armenia, and particularly throughout the regions of Ani and Van.

This website is an outstanding resource for information about the architectural history, and the recent reconstruction, of the Armenian sites at Ani and Aghtamar. The site also contains extensive information about other Armenian churches in Western Armenia.

Visit the website at *www.VirtualAni.org*

VISITING ANI TODAY

The historic walled city of Ani has a circumference of roughly five kilometers, and most of the historic sites can be reached without difficulty by walking on the unpaved footpaths that traverse the site.

Ani is uninhabited. A small village has developed just north of Ani, and there's a modest restaurant and a souvenir stand nearby, but there are no accommodations for travelers. To visit Ani, most visitors will choose to use the nearby city of Kars as a base.

At time of research there were no restrictions on traveling to Ani, and there were no restrictions on walking to any of the areas within the walled city of Ani. A fence surrounds the perimeter of the city and clearly marks the areas outside Ani that are closed to visitors. Do not go beyond this fence to areas that are close to, or abutting, the international border with Armenia.

Resist the temptation to wade across the shallow **Akhurian River** and into neighboring Armenia. The Turkey-Armenia border is closed, and the two countries don't have diplomatic relations, so an attempted crossing would be a serious international incident, and would certainly interrupt your travels.

Photographing Ani is no longer prohibited. This is a marked departure from the recent past. Still, it is advisable to avoid overtly photographing military sites such as the frontier guard towers in Armenia, or any Turkish soldiers who may be in the area.

For the best photography, plan your visit so that you arrive at Ani early in the morning. This will allow you to photograph the site with the walls of Ani in the background. Ani is gated, and entry is generally not possible earlier than 9 am, but it is worth the effort to try to get in early. Ani is not crowded at any hour of day, but in early morning you are apt to have the entire place to yourself. In early evening, just before sunset, you will be able to photograph the site with the hills of Armenia in the background. If you go in the afternoon during the summer, you might bump into some other travelers, too.

To get there, from Kars you must take a private taxi. There is no regularly scheduled transportation from Kars to Ani. Negotiate the fare in advance. You can expect to pay 120 Turkish Lira (about $60) for a round trip fare, which includes having the taxi wait for three hours. Pay a bit more for a longer stay. Travel time from Kars to Ani is about 35 minutes.

The City Walls

The massive **City Walls** that you see upon arrival at Ani were built by the Armenian King Smbat II in AD 978. The construction of these walls offers strong evidence that Ani must have been growing rapidly in population under the reign of the Bagratunis.

Formerly restricted area at Ani

This is because Ani already had a set of defensive walls when the Bagratunis relocated their capital to Ani seventeen years earlier in AD 961. Those original walls protected a much smaller area of land, however, and were located near the citadel.

When the Bagratunis relocated their capital to Ani, the city's defensive walls had extended across only the narrowest part of the bluff of land upon which Ani is built, and had protected only the citadel. The new outer walls built in AD 978 thus represented a geographic expansion of the area of Ani under protection.

Even these new outer walls may not have enclosed an area large enough to contain all of Ani's 100,000 residents during the peak of its population in the eleventh century. H. F. B. Lynch observed during his travels to Ani in 1893 that many of Ani's residents must have lived outside the walls.

The caves surrounding Ani, as well as the plain north of the city, may have served this purpose, perhaps for Ani's least wealthy classes. The ruins of Armenian churches in the plain outside Ani further supports the theory that Ani was too big for its walls.

Ani's new defensive perimeter consisted of double walls with staggered gates. If an invading force was able to get past the first outer wall, the invading army would be confronted with another tall wall. They would then have to make a sharp turn, and run down an alley, to reach the next gate at the inner wall. The resulting delay and confusion would give an advantage to the defenders of Ani.

The inner wall is interrupted at intervals with tall defensive towers. Some of the towers bear inscriptions in Armenian from the twelfth and thirteenth centuries, which showed that they had been built by private individuals as memorials to themselves.

The City Walls

The ruins of a tower at Ani

The Gates of Ani

The **Lion Gate** is the main entrance that visitors use today for access to Ani, and it is believed to have also been the primary gate for the city during the eleventh century. The gate takes its name from the bass relief of a lion that is set in the wall near this gate.

The **Kars Gate** is located west of the Lion Gate (on the right, when facing the gate from outside) and is not often used by visitors to Ani today. This gate is flanked by two large towers that are linked by an arch. A large cross is set in stone near this gate. The **Checkerboard Gate** is sited east of the Lion Gate (on the left, when facing the gate from outside), and earned its name because the wall here features a pattern of black and red stones that are arranged as a checkerboard.

The Akhurian River Bridge

Nearly one thousand years ago, a bridge spanned the **Akhurian River** and linked Ani with the lands of Armenian kingdoms farther east in Lori.

Today the Akhurian River forms part of the international frontier between Turkey and Armenia, and the border between the two countries is closed. The arched roadway of the bridge has collapsed, and only the two abutments of the bridge are still standing.

The broken bridge is a powerful symbol of the broken link between Armenia's eastern and western provinces. The bridge illustrates, as well, that Ani is stranded on the wrong side of history: it is located just beyond the reach of the people for whom it represents their national identity.

The bridge had probably been erected by the thirteenth century, although some sources suggest a construction date that is a century or two earlier—perhaps as early as the tenth century.

A gateway to the bridge bore the inscription of the year 1320 according to Lynch. Fragments of other inscriptions nearby bore the dates of 1256 and 1310. The ruins of a covered staircase leading to the bridge exist today, and pass close to the **Monastery of the Virgins,** which stands on a bluff above the river.

The ruins of the bridge stand directly on each side of the international border, and direct access is therefore prohibited. The Monastery of the Virgins, located on a bluff above the Akhurian River, just north of the bridge, provides a good vantage point for viewing and photographing the bridge.

The Ani Cathedral

The **Ani Cathedral** is the grandest and most stately of the surviving churches of Ani. This is a structure of great importance in Armenian history, and also a building that made a great contribution to the development of the world's architecture.

Construction of the Cathedral was begun in AD 989 by King Smbat II and was completed more than a decade later, in AD 1010, according to an inscription written in ancient Armenian on the southern face of the building.

The inscription states that in the year 1010, during the reign of Gagik, the King of Kings of Armenia and Georgia, the Cathedral, which had been founded by King Smbat, was completed by Katranideh, Queen of Armenia and daughter of the King of Siunik, at the bidding of her husband, King Gagik.

There's no reference to the Cathedral's architect on any of the surviving inscriptions, but we know from other records that this was the work of Trdat, a revered architect who is also credited with having erected the monasteries of Marmashen, Sanahin, and Haghpat, which are all located in today's Armenia. Trdat is also credited with the repair of the dome of the Hagia Sophia in today's Istanbul.

The Ani Cathedral is in the form of a domed basilica, and originally featured the traditional Armenian drum and conical dome that have become the hallmarks of Armenian ecclesiastical architecture.

The Cathedral of Ani

The drum and dome are now gone and there is a gaping hole in the roof where they once stood.

Some sources indicate that the dome collapsed as early as 1319, following an earthquake. Whether Ani suffered damage from this ancient earthquake is disputed, however. Other sources report that most of the drum supporting the dome collapsed during another earthquake in the 1800s. Regardless of the date of the collapse, we know that the dome was missing at the time of H. F. B. Lynch's expedition to Ani in 1893.

The Cathedral has suffered damage more recently from a 1988 earthquake, and from the blasting of explosives in 2000 and 2001 at the quarry located just across the Akhurian River, in Armenia.

Some experts believe that the Cathedral's interior, which has many of the characteristics of the Gothic style of architecture, established the Cathedral as the origin of this architectural style. When the Ani Cathedral was completed in the early eleventh century, the Romanesque style of architecture was universal in Europe. The pointed arches and coupled piers that appear in the Ani Cathedral are the precursors of Gothic architecture—a style that would not appear in Europe for another two hundred years.

Today the interior walls of the Cathedral have been whitewashed and defaced in many places. The whitewash covers Armenian frescoes and has been spread there recently, during the period of Turkish custody of this site.

On still other parts of the interior walls, there are gaps in the façade indicating places where Armenian *khatchkars* (stone crosses) had once been on display. Other Armenian inscriptions have in recent years been covered with paint, with the apparent intention of concealing from visitors the Armenian history of the Cathedral.

Whitewashed or not, there is no dispute that this is an Armenian cathedral of great significance. In the words of H. F. B. Lynch, it is "a monument of the highest artistic merit, denoting a standard of culture which was far in advance of the contemporary standards in the West."

The interior of the Cathedral of Ani

The Cathedral of Ani

The Church of the Redeemer

The **Church of the Redeemer** is perhaps the most iconic structure at Ani today. The building stands in isolation near the eastern edge of the city, a short walk from the Cathedral. All the structures that once surrounded this church have long since fallen.

The building is also known as the **Church of the Savior**, and by its Armenian name, **Soorp Prkitch**.

The iconic stature of this monument is enhanced by its unlikely appearance. Half the building collapsed roughly sixty years ago, following a storm. All that remains today of the Church of the Redeemer is half of its exterior shell. The interior is now exposed to the world as if it was an egg that was cracked into two pieces—one still standing, one forever lost.

In 1901, roughly sixty years before its partial collapse, Lynch had prophetically warned that the building "will not endure for many years longer, unless steps be taken to save it from falling in."

Construction of the church was completed in AD 1035, shortly after the completion of the Cathedral. According to an inscription on its walls, its construction was linked to the acquisition by an Armenian prince of a fragment of the cross upon which Jesus had been crucified.

The inscription says that in the year 1035, the prince Aplgharib, having journeyed to Constantinople by order of King Smbat, the King of Kings, obtained with great difficulty and at considerable expense a piece of the Holy Cross. Upon his return, he built this church and directed that nightly services should be held until the return of Christ.

Although the base of the church appears to have a circular design, on closer inspection it is actually a 19-sided polygon that approximates the appearance of a circle. The circular drum that sits on this base is, by contrast, a perfect circle with 24 blind arcades, half of which are pierced by narrow windows. The result is a design that creates geometric, engineering, and architectural difficulties.

The Church of the Redeemer

Diane Favro, a Professor of Architecture at the University of California at Los Angeles, writes extensively about the design of this church in the book *Armenian Kars and Ani*, and provides some answers, none conclusive, to the riddle of why anyone would design such a geometrically complex building.

Numerical symbolism may have contributed to the selection of the 19-sided polygon for the base and to the decision to top the base with a circular drum that is "pierced" with 12 narrow windows. The numbers of the Armenian calendar may have also contributed to the design decisions for this structure.

Ultimately, concludes the architect Favro, the only thing that can truly be verified about the design of the church is that it all stems from the decision to honor a relic of the True Cross. This relic of the cross upon which Jesus was crucified may have prompted the selection of a centralized plan reminiscent of both a tomb and a martyrium.

The Church of Soorp Grigor of Tigran Honents

The **Church of Soorp Grigor (St. Gregory) of Tigran Honents** is so named because it was commissioned to be built by a wealthy merchant named Tigran Honents, in honor of St. Gregory the Illuminator, the founder of the Armenian Church.

This church is just a few meters from the Church of the Redeemer, and is perched at the edge of the bluff that leads to the Akhurian River.

Construction was completed in AD 1215, as attested by an inscription written in Armenian script on an exterior wall of the building. The inscription recites that in the year 1215, during the government of Zakare, one Tigran, of the family of Honents, built the monastery upon this site in the hope that his good work would bring long life to his House and to the son of Zakare.

This is one of the most significant structures from Ani's Zakarian period, which was a period of renewed prosperity for the city. Many rich merchants made significant gifts to the Armenian Church during this time, and the Church of Soorp Grigor is one of the finest examples of this benevolence.

The church was notable in its day, and also now, for the beautiful frescoes that adorn all of its interior walls. In recent years these frescoes have undergone considerable damage from vandalism, and from an intentional whitewashing performed by the current custodians of the site.

One entire section of frescoes was chipped from the walls and destroyed, apparently during the 1990s when a Turkish professor was performing excavations at Ani. The Virtual Ani project concludes that achieving this level of destruction must have taken considerable time, and must have required the use of scaffolds or ladders.

Just one hundred years ago, H. F. B. Lynch had been able to write about this church, that upon "entering the building we are at once impressed by its almost perfect preservation; the plaster adheres to the walls and ceilings, and the frescoes with which they were adorned are still intelligible. Yet here we have a monument erected nearly 800 years ago, and which has not yet been touched by a restorer's hand." Much of this historic artwork has been lost during the century after 1915.

The Monastery of the Virgins

The tiny **Monastery of the Virgins** stands on a rocky bluff just above the Akhurian River, and is hidden from the view of most of the plateau of Ani.

This monastery stands almost directly on the current international border of Turkey and Armenia, and access to it has therefore been restricted for many years. The area has long been classified as a military zone.

Beginning in 2013, however, travelers have been allowed to climb down to the monastery without any restriction of access. Traveling beyond this monastery, to the riverbank, is still prohibited.

The monastery is a short distance from the Church of Soorp Grigor of Tigran Honents, and requires a bit of sure-footedness to reach because of its location on a promontory that is mid-way between the plateau of Ani, and the Akhurian River.

The Monastery of the Virgins is sometimes referred to as the Monastery of the Hripsimian Virgins. The name is derived from the virgin martyrs of St. Hripsime and it is believed that the monastery may have been occupied by nuns.

The surviving building probably dates back to the eleventh century. There are no inscriptions on its walls, and therefore no attestation of the building date.

The roof above the drum of the surviving chapel of the Monastery of the Virgins is multi-gabled, and resembles a half-closed umbrella or an accordion. This is the only surviving example of a roof of this style at Ani, and experts believe that this architectural style, seen in other Armenian churches, may have originated here.

The Chapel of Soorp Grigor

The **Chapel of Soorp Grigor (St. Gregory)** stakes a solitary stand near the walls of Ani, roughly 1,000 meters northwest of the Church of Soorp Grigor (St. Gregory) of Tigran Honents.

Observers have praised this chapel as a charming little monument, and this charm is abundant both when viewed from a distance and also upon closer inspection. The chapel is estimated to have been constructed in the tenth century and its nearly circular design, topped by a smaller, and circular, drum, has prompted comparisons to the design of the Church of the Holy Redeemer.

Frescoes from a more recent era, perhaps from the thirteenth century, are visible on the interior walls. There has been an attempt at preservation here during the past decade, and there's been destruction, as well. Graves in an adjoining sepulcher were desecrated by treasure hunters in 1998.

Other Important Sites at Ani

One of the tragedies of Ani is that far more of its Armenian cultural sites have been lost than have been preserved. The sites described above are the best preserved of Ani. The tragic state of Ani's preservation is perhaps most strongly-illustrated by the observation that the broken shell of the Church of the Holy Redeemer deserves to be counted in the list above as one of Ani's best-preserved Armenian sites.

Many of the easily overlooked sites of Ani are located within the city's **Inner Fortress**, an area that is also known as the **Citadel**. The Citadel of Ani is located on a hilltop near the southern end of the city, and its elevation is unsurpassed by any location with the city walls. This is the area of Ani that was protected by walls at the time the Bagratuni Dynasty located its capital here in AD 961. The vantage from the Citadel allows a view of all of the city of Ani below.

The ruins of the **Palace of the Citadel** and of several buildings and churches are visible within the confines of the Citadel. The Palace of the Citadel was the residence of the Bagratuni Dynasty while they ruled Ani. The Palace was excavated by the archaeologist Nicholas (Nikolai) Marr beginning in 1892.

The **Church of the Citadel Palace** is also located here, although just barely. Only one wall of this church is still standing. This is a historically significant church dating at least from the earliest time of the Bagratuni Dynasty, and possibly earlier. Marr identified this church as the oldest surviving church at Ani. Even if this designation was accurate, the destruction of the past century has certainly removed this church from the category of "surviving" structures.

The ruins of the **Mausoleum of the Child Princes** are located just southeast of the Palace of the Citadel. The drum and dome of this structure are believed to have been standing as recently as the 1960s, but collapsed during an earthquake in 1966.

The **Hexagonal Church of the Citadel** is at the far southern end of the Citadel. As indicated by its name, the church has six sides. As with so many of Ani's churches, the dome and most of the drum of the Hexagonal Church have fallen.

This church may have been erected as early as the tenth century. The stones of the exterior façade suggest a substantial renovation was completed some time later, perhaps in the thirteenth or fourteenth century.

If you have walked as far as the Hexagonal Church, then from here you have an excellent view of the **Maiden's Castle**. Most visitors will need to be content with simply viewing the Maiden's Castle from this location. Hiking out to its location, on a promontory at the extreme end of Ani, will take three or four hours for the round trip.

This promontory has been closed to the public for many years. At time of research the area was restricted, as well, and was located beyond a chain link fence that encircles the publicly accessible areas of Ani.

I was able to hike about halfway to the promontory in about one hour, but did not complete the trek because of the military's restriction on access.

Hexagonal Church

The Maiden's Castle is also sometimes called the **Virgin's Castle**. Local people may know the area by the Turkish names **Kizkale** or **Kiz Kalesi**. The site has never been excavated, and one supposes that, because of its remote location, it may not have been plundered, either.

On the plain of Ani, near the northern walls, the ruins of **King Gagik's Church of Soorp Grigor (St. Gregory)** are evident. This is yet another church dedicated to the founder of the Armenian Church, Soorp Grigor Lusavorich (St. Gregory the Illuminator). This building is sometimes called the millennium church because it was erected sometime between AD 990 and 1000.

The building had the same wedding cake design as the legendary Zvartnots Cathedral, which is also in ruins and is located near Echmiadzin in today's Republic of Armenia. The Ani version of

Soorp Arakelots (Church of the Holy Apostles)

the famous Zvartnots closely resembled the cathedral of Zvartnots in one additional important way: it was equally unstable.

King Gagik's Church of Soorp Grigor was reinforced with added masonry not more than 20 years after it was originally completed. The reinforcements didn't help. The church collapsed shortly thereafter.

The ruins were lost for a time, buried by layers of the city's history. Marr's excavations uncovered the lost church in 1906, however. An account of his excavation is detailed in the book that Marr published about Ani many years later.

During the course of these excavations, Marr uncovered a large statue of a man holding a model of the church. The statute was broken and in fragments. When Marr reassembled it, the statue turned out to be a bit larger than life, measuring more than seven feet tall. The statue honored a man who was a bit larger than life, himself. This monument was the **Statue of King Gagik**.

Marr displayed the statue, along with other artifacts that he had uncovered, in a small museum that he set up in a mosque within the city of Ani. The museum was looted when Ani was captured from Armenia in 1920, and the statue was either lost or destroyed at this time, too. Years later, a fragment from the priceless statue—the left arm—turned up in the Erzerum Archaeological Museum, where it is now on display.

A so-called **Fire Temple** of Ani is believed by some to be a Zoroastrian temple at which the faithful worshipped fire, as early as the first century AD, until perhaps the fourth century. If this is accurate, then this temple is the most significant building at Ani from before the Christian era. Others theorize that the so-called Fire Temple might actually be an early Christian monument from the middle of the fourth century.

The **Church of the Holy Apostles**, which is known to Armenians as **Soorp Arakelots**, is an historically significant site that is today in a state of ruin, partly because of the intentional vandalism committed by the current custodians of Ani.

The church was erected during the dynasty of the Pahlavid family and an inscription on one of its walls reveals that an endowment or gift was made to the church in 1031 by Apughamir, one of the princes of the Pahlavid family.

The Church of the Holy Apostles was excavated and studied by Marr in 1909. Parts of his reconstruction were deliberately destroyed sometime after 1921.

A single wall of a building known as the **Georgian Church** is standing today, supported by metal braces that appear to have been installed mostly for appearances sake.

The hideously "restored" **Merchant's Palace** is a site that you will want to avoid, unless you wish to observe poor reconstruction methods. The building dated from the twelfth or thirteenth century, and one theory contends that this was the residential palace of the merchant Tigran Honents. A so-called restoration in 1999 resulted in a massive rebuilding of the site, using new materials. As a result, the site was destroyed, rather than preserved.

The **Mosque of Minuchir**, known in Turkish as the **Menucehr Camii**, is the subject of dueling histories. Armenians contend that the building was originally a palace from the Bagratid period and that it was later converted to a mosque after the Turkish conquest of Ani. Turks contend that the building was always a mosque, that it was erected just after the Turks captured Ani, and that it is therefore the oldest surviving Turkish mosque in today's Turkey.

Beginning in 1906, the archaeologist Nicholas (Nikolai) Marr used the mosque as a museum for the relics and artifacts that he had unearthed during his excavations of Ani. The museum was looted in 1920 after Turkey invaded Armenia and annexed Ani.

The Cave City of Ani

Chambers have been cut into the hills surrounding Ani, and these chambers, which resemble natural caves, are older than Ani. As many as 2,000 people may have lived in these caves, starting long before Ani was settled, and continuing as recently as the twentieth century.

Although most of the chambers were residences or were used for storage, some of these man-made caves served religious functions. An expedition from one century ago counted 30 chapels or churches and more than 800 chambers. A more recent survey was completed in 2004 by a team of Italian researchers.

Underground Ani

Ani extended underground, as well. An entire underground city is believed to have existed at Ani, long before Ani achieved its fame. This underworld included residences, tunnels, and rooms.

Some of these subterranean rooms may have served as monk cells. Researchers base this belief upon the discovery in these areas of parchments bearing Armenian script. Researchers say the messages on the parchments suggest that they were communications between monks who were studying religion.

These parchments were dated to the sixth and seventh centuries and suggest that there had been an Armenian monastery here hundreds of years before the Bagratids had selected Ani as their capital.

Researchers discussed their analysis of the underground city during an international conference in 2014 in the nearby city of Kars.

The Church of the Shepherd

The **Church of the Shepherd** may have been constructed as early as the tenth century, and had managed to survive in a state of ruin until the start of the twentieth century. An earthquake in 1966 completed its destruction.

Today, one can view the rubble of this monument from the side of the Kars to Ani roadway, at a distance of several hundred meters northwest of the city of Ani. This is an area that is used by the military and which is therefore closed to the public.

The name Church of the Shepherd is derived from a fable that a shepherd built the church for his wife. According to this folklore, the shepherd's wife had complained that the churches of Ani were noisy and crowded.

*The Chapel of Soorp Grigor
as it appeared in 2003 before restoration*

NORTH OF ANI

The Monastery of Horomos

The ruins of the historically significant Armenian monastery of Horomos is located just north of Ani. The monastery, which is also known as **Koshavank**, was founded as early as AD 943, a few years before the Bagratid dynasty established its capital at Ani.

The site was already an important religious and cultural site when it was built during the reign of King Abas. Horomos rose further in stature a few years later, in AD 961, when the Bagratids moved the capital of their royal kingdom to nearby Ani.

The ruins of Horomos are located about 15 kilometers northeast of Ani, along the banks of the Akhurian River, directly on the border with today's Republic of Armenia.

H. F. B. Lynch visited Horomos in 1893 and described its monuments as "examples of the Armenian style at its very best."

Horomos had been renovated earlier in the nineteenth century, before Lynch's visit, and it was a functioning religious site until 1920, when Turkey seized the region from Armenia.

The Virtual Ani project describes the past century of Turkish custody as having been unkind to Horomos: "Some buildings have entirely vanished, and most of the surviving walls have been stripped of facing masonry." The dome of one of the monastic churches collapsed, sometime in the 1970s.

Gaining access to this site may be difficult today, for reasons of politics, as well as the terrain. Pilgrims who have attempted to visit speculate that the current custodians do not want the world to see the destruction that they have brought to Horomos. There are also no major roads to the site.

To get there, travel 15 kilometers northeast of Ani. **GPS map coordinates** for Horomos: 40 31' 11" N, 43 37' 45" E

Church of Karmir Vank

In the same region as Horomos, also roughly 15 kilometers north of Ani, the church of **Karmir Vank** remains in good condition. Visitors to the site will be rewarded with views of a church that is an important part of Armenian architectural and ecclesiastical history and which is an ideal representation of medieval Armenian church architecture.

The English translation of the name Karmir Vank is Red Church, or Red Monastery, which refers to the color of the building's stonework. The Turkish name that is widely used is **Kizil Kilise** and it is the Turkish name that travelers should use when asking for directions and for entry to the building.

Karmir Vank may date back to the tenth century, and it is believed to have been in use as a church until 1920 when the area was seized from Armenia by Turkey. The church is today used as a barn.

Horomos as it appeared in 2008
Photo by Samvel Karapetyan, Courtesy of Research on Armenian Architecture Foundation

Horomos as it appeared 100 years ago
Photographer Unknown

KARS PROVINCE

(Tandzor)

(Khask'euy)

(Ignidzor)   GRENADERSKOE (ZARISHAT)   Kaps   Ortakilisa   Toparli   Kaltakhchi   Kurs

(Olor)   Panaskert   (Okam)   Novo-Petrovka   Magaradzhik   Am

Okane   Olshanka   Kizil dali   ALEKSANDROPOL (GYUMRI)

Mananoglu   Novo-Pokrovka   Romanovo   Spasovka   KIZIL CHAKCHAK   Aleksandrovka

Mardenek   Malaia   Karakilisa

Top-dash   Voronstsovka   Romanovka   Balandur   Bash-Shuragel

(Vagover)   Bash kadiklar   Aguzum

Peniak   Arsenik   Gamar Vardan   (Haram)   Mevrek   Bairakhdar

(Banak)   Blagodarnoe   KARS   Subatan   (Aghin)   Artik

(Kosor)   Dzhala

Berdik   (Giarmali)   Petrovka   Novo-Estonskoe   Dovshan   Kizil-kilisa (Koshavank / Horomos)

(Sigdasor)   (Kiamkas)   Vladikars   Azat   Bazardzhik   Ani   Alageoz 4090 / 13419

(Avdost)   Amed   Aleksandrovka   Kizil-kala   Magasberd

Novo-Mikhailovka   Alam

Kars   Verishen   Besh Kilise (Khtzkonk)   (Tashnik)   Talin (T'alin)

Chermuk   (Chermayr)   TEKOR (DIGOR)   Mren   Talish (T'alish)

Partiz   (Boyal)   Novo-Selon   (Akriuk)

(Ch'atakh)   (Zibni)

(Metsrats)   Ali Safi   Iaglisa   Nakhichevan   [Bagaran]

2847 / 9341   SARIKAMISH   2969 / 9741

Enikeoy   (S. Khach')   (Kechvan)   (K'ers)   Pakran   [Ervandashat]

(Sirbasan)   2904 / 9528   Sardarapat   Markara

(Abulvart)   Khandere   Ala Dag   [Armavir]   Dzhanfida

(Getik)   Kot   3134 / 10282   Dzhafarabad   Igdalu

Upper Medzhinkert   Kavakend   Araks   Kulp   Surmalu   Karakala Br.

(Verin Mzhnkert)   Kagisman   KAGISMAN   (Koghb)   Pirlu   Karakala   Kiulluk

Lower Medzhinkert   Bash Kiul   (KAGHSVAN)   Chinchavat   Kamishlu   Blur

(Nerk'in Mzhnkert)   (Bashkeuy)   (K'aravank')   (Trapanek')   Suki   Karbulakh   Obi

(Short'i)   Agarag   Verin Charukhchi   Iaidzhi   IGDIR

KARAIURT   (Engija)   (Gomik)   (Hovasur)   Pirsakh   Igdirmava

Kazan   Sogutlu   Khoshkhabar   Khalfalu

Akkilisa   Ashagi   Molla-Kamar   Sultanaba

3276 / 10748   Surmalu

Abas-Geol   Orgov

L. Balik

Courtesy of Robert H. Hewsen

Scale

0   25km

0   25mi

- ◎ Vilayet (Province) Capital
- ◎ Sanjak (County) Capital
- ◎ Kaza (District) Center
- • Russian Sectarian Village
- † Armenian Bishop
- Armenian Catholic Vicar
- ♦ Armenian Monastery

Kars

A BRIEF HISTORY OF KARS

Before they packed up and moved their capital to Ani in AD 961, the Bagratid dynasty of Armenia had been centered at **Kars**. For thirty years, from AD 928 until AD 961, Kars was the capital of the Bagratid Kingdom of Armenia.

It is not likely that the Bagratids had viewed Kars as just a temporary way station prior to their move to Ani. If this had been the case, one expects that they would not have committed the resources to initiate the construction of buildings such as the mighty **Church of the Apostles**, an imposing structure that still stands today in the center of the city of Kars.

Construction of this magnificent church was begun in AD 943 by the Bagratid King Abbas I, and was completed roughly 25 years later. By the time the monument was completed, the Bagratids had moved to Ani, and Kars had become a separate Armenian kingdom known as **Vannad**, which is the Armenian name for the region of Kars.

Kars was ceded to the Byzantines in AD 1064, and then promptly captured by Turks in AD 1071. During the centuries that followed, Kars was a battleground between competing powers and was conquered and ruled by a succession of Turks, Georgians, and Mongols. The population for many years had a majority of Armenians.

Kars was incorporated into the Ottoman Turkish Empire in 1534 and for many years enjoyed a great deal of autonomy from its distant rulers. The region ultimately would become a contested frontier between the Ottoman and Russian Empires. The Russians briefly occupied Kars in 1828, and again in 1855. The Russians returned in 1878. This last time, they stayed for about 40 years.

The Modern Era

Kars, as a frontier region between two empires, was contested by the Turks and the Russians in the nineteenth century, but it had never been one of the Armenian provinces of the Ottoman Empire. In modern times, the region of Kars had been part of the Russian Empire until March, 1918.

Kars, as well as Ani, was part of the first Republic of Armenia from 1918 to 1920. Kars is therefore identified by Armenians as part of historic *Eastern* Armenia.

The history of those thousand days, when Kars was incorporated into the first Republic of Armenia, and then lost to Turkey, is a history that Armenians recall with heartbreak. Here's what happened.

By treaty with Turkey on March 3, 1918, the Russians had ceded Kars to Turkey, and the Turkish army had occupied Kars shortly thereafter, on April 25, 1918.

The Turkish army didn't stop after occupying Kars. It also marched across the Akhurian River to Alexandropol (today's Gyumri) and occupied that city.

Turkey then marched across Armenia, which in 1918 was a land that had become overwhelmed by refugees from the genocide.

In late May, 1918, Armenia stopped Turkey's advance at **Sardarapat**—a victory that prevented Turkey from reaching Yerevan. This victory is credited with saving the Armenian nation from annihilation.

By the end of 1918, Turkey, as one of the defeated powers of the Great War, was compelled by the Western Allies to withdraw its forces from Armenia. Within months, on April 28, 1919, Kars had been united with the Republic of Armenia. Armenian soldiers stood guard at the fortress of Kars.

They didn't stand guard there for long. Armenia held the fortress, and Kars, for barely more than one year.

The defeated Turkish army of World War I, under the leadership of both Mustafa Kemal (Kemal Attaturk) and of his commander on Turkey's eastern front, General Kiazim Karabekir, invaded Kars and captured the fortress on October 30, 1920. The entire Armenian population of Kars fled, mostly to Alexandropol.

By the end of 1920, Soviet rule had been imposed upon Armenia, and Turkey had annexed the entire province of Kars, as well as of **Mt. Ararat**, the biblical mountain whose twin peaks are the *mayr* and *hayr* — the mother and father — of the Armenian nation.

The Russians and the Turks ratified these changes the following year in a pair of treaties named for Moscow and Kars. Armenia wasn't a party to either agreement.

The Treaty of Kars allowed for the deportation from Kars of any of its remaining Armenians. A decade later, Kars was nearly deserted and had a population of only a few hundred people. By 2010, the population had grown to more than 73,000.

The Near Demise of Armenia

According to the British historian and author **Christopher J. Walker**, if in 1918 the Armenians had not defeated the invading Turks at Sardarapat, "it is perfectly possible that the word Armenia would have henceforth denoted only an antique geographical term."

VISITING KARS TODAY

Traveling to Kars directly from Armenia was once a simple matter. A border crossing operated for years between Kars and the Armenian city of Gyumri. The Turkey-Armenia border has been closed since 1993, however.

To get to Kars overland from Armenia one must now travel through Georgia, which adds at least one full day to the journey. Traveling by air is simpler, although more expensive. There are several flights each day between Istanbul and Kars.

The Castle of Kars

The **Castle of Kars**, which is also called the Kars Citadel, looms above the modern city of Kars from a hilltop at the northern edge of town. The Turkish name for the Castle is **Kars Kalesi**.

Some of the walls of the Castle date back to the era of the Bagratid dynasty more than 1,000 years ago, but there has been extensive reconstruction and building over the centuries.

It is with a heavy heart that most Armenians visit or view this castle. The fortress was held by Armenia during the period of the first Republic of Armenia from 1918 to 1920, and it fell to the invading Turkish army in 1920. The loss of the fortress has been called one of the most ignoble defeats in Armenian military history.

The commander of the invading Turkish army had ordered a full-scale assault on the fortress on October 30, 1920. This assault had been delayed by three days because of heavy Armenian resistance.

Soorp Arakelots,
The Church of the Holy Apostles

Richard G. Hovannisian described the battle in the book *Armenian Kars and Ani*. "There was still a little fighting spirit left among some of the Armenian troops who slowed the Turkish advance, but by noon Turkish uniforms were spotted on the commanding height" of the fort.

Shortly afterward, "the civilian Armenian population came under fire when they tried to flee Kars. A few final volleys were heard from the Armenian artillery before everything fell silent." The fortress had fallen after about three hours of battle. The Armenians retreated to Alexandropol (today's Gyumri).

Yeghishe Charents

The Armenian writer, poet, and political activist **Yeghishe Charents** was born Yeghishe Soghomonyan in Kars in 1897. He lived there until 1915, and then again from 1919 to 1920. He served in the defense of Van in 1915 during the Armenian Genocide and he survived to become one of Armenia's most celebrated poets.

Charents is the author of **Erkir Nayiri (Land of Nayiri)**, a novel in which he mourns, and attempts to make sense of, the loss of Kars.

Charents died in Yerevan in 1937 after being imprisoned during Stalin's Great Purge. He had been discovered to have written a secret hidden message in one of his poems. The message said "Oh, Armenian people, your only salvation is your collective power."

He was "rehabilitated" some 20 years later. The Soviet Union commemorated him with a postage stamp in 1958 and Armenia did the same in 1997 on the centennial anniversary of his birth. Today the 1,000-dram denomination of Armenian currency features his likeness.

The Yerevan home of Charents was converted to a house museum in 1975. The home of his childhood in Kars is unmarked and is in ruins.

The Church of the Apostles

The *Armenian Church of the Apostles*, which is also known by the Armenian name **Soorp Arakelots**, was built during the Bagratid era. Construction started in AD 943, and was probably completed within about 25 years, by about the year AD 967, which is shortly after the Bagratids had moved their capital to Ani. The building stands today in excellent condition near the foot of the Kars Castle.

Twelve human figures are carved in low relief on the drum of the church. Some sources indicate that 11 of these human figures represent the apostles, and that one represents St. Gregory the Illuminator. Under this theory, the apostle Judas is not featured. Another source reports that the 12 figures represent all 12 apostles, one of which has an ugly face. Presumably this is the face of Judas.

By most accounts, the figure that is carved on the drum directly above the western entrance represents St. Gregory. This figure is accompanied by a pair of snakes, or serpents. These serpents are probably intended as a reference to St. Gregory's many years of confinement in a snake-filled pit.

This Armenian church has seen many uses during its thousand-year history. The building was constructed as an Armenian church, and this is how it was used exclusively during the first 100 years of its existence. After the Seljuk Turkish conquest of Kars in 1064 the building was converted to use as a mosque, then abandoned, and then used as a mosque again in 1579 after the establishment of Ottoman rule over Kars.

The building was returned to use as a church in 1878, although not by the Armenians. The Russians had just conquered Kars, and so they converted the building to use as a Russian Orthodox church. Thus began an era in which the function of the church was changed many more times, by a succession of new custodians.

In 1919, during the period of the first Armenian Republic, the building was restored to its intended use as an Armenian church. This status lasted until the Turkish capture of Kars at the end of the following year. The Turks converted the church to a mosque (again) and then refitted it as a storage depot, and then a museum, and then, once again, as a mosque.

Visitors to the church today will find it operating as a mosque. The inside has been refitted for use as a mosque, but the exterior still honors, through those carved reliefs on the church drum, St. Gregory the Illuminator and eleven of Christ's apostles. A bell tower, similar in appearance to the bell tower at Haghpat, in today's Armenia, stood beside the church for many years, but was destroyed sometime after 1920.

The Kars Museum

The anthropological museum of Kars is worth a short visit if you have a spare hour, but this will not be a priority for most travelers. The greatest attraction of the museum is a pair of engraved wooden doors that were removed from an Armenian church.

The doors feature an elaborately engraved Armenian cross, part of which has been defaced to conceal its Christian nature. The exhibit does not identify the doors as Armenian and offers no explanation of their historic significance.

Villager at Mren

SOUTH OF KARS

The Cathedral of Mren

The **Cathedral of Mren** stands a lonely, solitary vigil at the center of a now desolate plateau that was once a thriving Armenian town. The cathedral was erected in AD 638 and through the centuries it has seen the surrounding Armenian region grow and flourish and decay and, after 1920, die.

The plateau has remained a barren waste for the entire century since the Armenians were expelled. Mren is today the last building standing, and it may not remain standing for much longer.

Mren became a subject of fleeting interest in the Armenian news media in 2013 when it was identified as being on the verge of collapse. Christina Maranci, Ph D, a professor of Armenian Art and Architecture, made the projection.

The church, which is more than 1,300 years old, was mostly intact until the time of the Turkish conquest of the area in 1920. There has been extensive damage since 1920, however. Most of the south side of the church fell in 2008, and Dr. Maranci reports that the foundation of the church is so badly undermined, that collapse could be imminent.

The imminent collapse of the church is not the result of decades of neglect, or the natural result of aging.

Mren, c. 100 years ago
Photographer Unknown

Mren, 2014

Instead, the damage is certainly the result of vandalism. Since 1920, the area around the foundation of the church has been excavated. The Virtual Ani project concludes, with justification, that this excavation is "sabotage intended to weaken the structure in order to encourage the church's 'natural' collapse."

The predictions about Mren's pending fate are accurate. If the cathedral's foundation is not restored, the entire structure could soon collapse under its own weight. If this happens, the current custodians would certainly characterize the loss as natural.

Mren is located in the Digor district of the region of Kars, approximately 34 kilometers south of Ani. The cathedral is sited just about one kilometer west of the Arpa River, which forms the international border between today's Turkey and Armenia.

Numerous sources report that Mren is in a military zone, and that access is not possible without permission from the military—an authorization that many sources also predict will not be forthcoming. I have read reports that state that the people in village nearest to Mren are under orders to turn visitors away.

Despite all of this, I was able to visit the site in 2014.

The drive from Kars to the village nearest to Mren took 75 minutes. Upon arrival in this neighboring village, we simply paid a local man to drive us in his tractor over the rough unpaved track to Mren. The 45-minute tractor ride covered a distance of about three kilometers, and we paid the man 150 Turkish Lira (about $75). We stayed at Mren for more than an hour. Nobody said anything about getting permission from the military.

I suspect that if we had attempted to walk to the cathedral, rather than pay for the tractor ride, that we might have been turned away. True or not, it was no matter. The track was rough, the sun was bright, and the heat was dry and intense. The tractor ride to Mren proved itself to be essential. The tractor might have also been good cover from the watchful eyes of soldiers who are stationed at a watchtower on a distant hill.

The Monastery of Khtzkonk

The **Monastery of Khtzkonk** is known to the region's locals by the Turkish name **Besh Kilise**. The name made sense until about one half century ago. The English translation of Besh Kilise is **Five Churches**, and for almost all of its existence, this monastery was the site of five churches.

Four of the monastery's five churches were destroyed by the Turkish Army during the 1950s, however. This was a period when some of the people in positions of authority in Turkey had resumed destroying the Armenian churches that had survived after 1915. The destruction was not in furtherance of some other project. There was no plan to build a shopping mall on the site, or a road, or a dam, or even a mosque. The churches were simply blown up, and the shrapnel from the structures was left as litter on the hillside.

From the original five churches of Five Churches, the sole surviving structure is the **Church of Soorp Sarkis**. This was the largest of the churches at this monastery and its architecture is historically noteworthy for, among other things, its umbrella shaped roof.

This roof design is also present on the surviving chapel of the Monastery of the Virgins, a thirteenth century structure at the nearby capital of Ani. The roof on Soorp Sarkis pre-dates the one at Ani by about two hundred years, however, making this perhaps the earliest surviving example of the umbrella, or accordion, roof on an Armenian church.

Soorp Sarkis is an example of architectural design that has become known as the Ani School of Armenian architecture. The quality of its construction exceeds anything that survives at Ani, however. Today, this spectacular masterpiece of architecture is at risk of imminent collapse.

More is probably known about the destruction of the churches of the Monastery of Khtzkonk than about the monastery's earliest use and construction. Inscriptions on the individual churches do

Khtzkonk Monastery, 2000
Photo by Samvel Karapetyan, Courtesy of
Research on Armenian Architecture Foundation

not offer evidence of the date when the monastic complex was founded. The inscriptions, most of them now destroyed, do offer information about the construction of the individual structures, one of which dates back to the seventh century. The monastery, one suspects, may be a bit older.

The most ancient of the four churches that was destroyed by the Turkish army during the 1950s is a structure that was originally constructed as early as the seventh century. Inscriptions on this building, the **Church of Soorp Hovhannes (St. John) the Baptist**, are dated to AD 1001 and mentioned Queen Katranideh of Ani, the wife of King Gagik.

The building was sited immediately south of the surviving church of Soorp Sarkis, which, on the accompanying photograph, is the church that is immediately left of Soorp Sarkis.

The second of the four churches that Turkey destroyed in the 1950s is the **Church of the Holy Mother of God**, which had been constructed in the tenth century. The Armenian name for the church was **Soorp Astvatsatsin**. This church was sited immediately south of the Soorp Hovhannes.

The third and fourth churches that Turkey destroyed are the **Church of Soorp Stephanos Nakhavka** and the **Church of Soorp Grigor Lusavorich (St. Gregory the Illuminator)**. Each of these structures dates back to the tenth and eleventh centuries. The Church of Soorp Stephanos Nakhavka was constructed on a rock spur just opposite Soorp Hovhannes.

The Church of Soorp Grigor Lusavorich (St. Gregory the Illuminator) stood apart from the other four churches, farther to the east on a separate rocky spur. There were ancient Armenian graves on the slope above this church until about one quarter century ago.

The Monastery of Khtzkonk was in use by the Armenians until 1920. After 1920 the Armenians were expelled and the region was declared a restricted military zone. One needed a special travel permit to enter this area, and to enter the nearby village of Digor.

This restriction continued for the next six or seven decades. Travel restrictions were finally eased during the 1990s and I was able to visit the site in 2014 without any restriction.

The churches of the monastery were destroyed during this period of restricted access. Physical evidence suggests that the destruction was caused by explosives. Shattered fragments from the individual churches are scattered in the surrounding hills, "flung far from their original positions," according to a report produced by the Virtual Ani project.

A foreign visitor to the monastery in 1959 was the first to observe and report that only one of the five churches was still standing, and that this one remaining church, Soorp Sarkis, was badly damaged. People living in nearby Digor acknowledged that the destruction had been wrought by Turkish soldiers. The estimated time of the destruction has since been narrowed to the period from 1955 to 1959 based upon interviews with nearby residents.

To get there, travel southwest from Kars for roughly 25 kilometers to the town of Digor. From Digor, the hike to Khtzkonk Monastery is about 45 minutes. This is a strenuous but uncomplicated hike. The Monastery of Khtzkonk and the Cathedral of Mren are both in the same region and a visit to both can be combined in a single day-trip from Kars. Mren is located a bit farther south of Digor.

GPS map coordinates for Cathedral of Mren: 40 14' 32" N, 43 39' 47" E. **GPS map coordinates** for Monastery of Khtzkonk: 40 22' 10" N, 43 24' 59" E

Tzarakar Monastery

Tzarakar Monastery is the most intriguing Armenian monastery that no one has ever heard of. The monastery dates back at least to the tenth century, was active for several hundred years, and then became first forgotten, and then lost. Only in the past few years has it been rediscovered.

It's easy to think of this site as simply a cave church, because that's all that's left of it today. But this would greatly oversimplify the matter, and would not do justice to the history and lost architecture of this fine site.

If you visit today, you'll see that caves and chambers were carved into the side of a mountain and served as some of the chapels for this monastery. The excavations form parts of the monastery, just as the excavations at Geghardt Monastery, in today's Republic of Armenia, supplemented the freestanding buildings there. But the freestanding buildings of Geghardt have survived. At Tzarakar, they are all gone. All that remains at Tzarakar today are the cave-churches that have been carved into the mountain. These excavations created six chapels and one cruciform-designed church.

Tzarakar certainly existed by AD 952, based on the existence of a dated inscription that survives on the western wall of its church. Scholars believe it probably existed well before that, too. The site is also mentioned in historical sources in AD 1186. But then there is almost no mention of Tzarakar for the next several centuries. The monastery is believed to have been ruined by 1830, after which it became completely forgotten to history.

Tzarakar was finally visited by a researcher in 1999. This visit is noteworthy as perhaps the first time the site was studied by experts, and as certainly the first time that anyone published anything about the location. In 2008, and again in 2010, a scientific expedition was carried out by the **Research on Armenian Architecture (RAA)** organization, headed by the architect and scholar **Samvel Karapetyan**.

The research published by Karapetyan acknowledges that the location of Tzarakar was unknown until recently, which he describes as five kilometers from the old Armenian town of Kechror. This town has been replaced today by the nearby town of Cukurayva, in the region of Kars. According to Karapetyan, the parts of the monastery that were carved into the side of the mountain survived, whereas the rest was lost, because the caves were too difficult to destroy.

The cave at Tzarakar Monastery
Photo by Bared Maronian

I visited the site in 2014. It is certainly out of the way, but not difficult to reach. This will probably be the lowest priority for most visitors to the Kars region, despite its historic significance.

Go to Tzarakar if you have already seen the other sites described in this chapter, and if you still have time. Allow a bit more than one half day for this visit.

To get there, travel 61 kilometers south of Kars, to the town of Cukurayva, which should take about 75 minutes. From the village, the hike to the site takes about 30 minutes. Once at the site, some moderate climbing is necessary, so wear hiking shoes. **GPS map coordinates** for Tzarakar: 40 14' 50.2" N, 42 54' 51.2" E

MT. ARARAT

Mt. Ararat is the spiritual heart of Armenia. The Armenians make a legendary claim that they are descendants of Noah, and so Ararat is central to Armenian self-identity. The mountain is depicted on Armenian currency, its postage stamps, and its peaks adorn the coat of arms of the Armenian Republic.

Ararat is the tallest mountain of historic Armenia, at 5,165 meters, and it soars in the national consciousness, as well. The mountain loomed large when National Geographic published an article about Armenia in 2004: "Armenians have been pondering Mount Ararat and its neighbor, Little Ararat, since the birth of civilization," according to their report.

Mt. Ararat, from Western Armenia

The mountain has been located within today's Turkey since 1920, and visitors who wish to hike to its peak will first need to travel to the town of **Dogubeyazit**, from which most expeditions depart.

The base of Ararat near the Araks River, which forms part of the border between Turkey and Armenia, was until 1840 the site of the Armenian monastery of **Soorp Hagop**. The monastery was located at an elevation of about 5,600 feet, some 2,900 feet above the plain, about one third of the way from the base of the mountain.

This monastery had been located in the Armenian village of **Akhury**, which was said to be the only village that had ever been located at such a high altitude on the mountain. Armenians chose this location for the village because it was believed that this was the place Noah first settled after departing from the Ark.

According to Armenian tradition, it was upon this site that Noah built an altar after his safe descent from the Ark. The church of the Monastery of Soorp Hagop was built upon the site of Noah's altar, and was constructed in the eighth or ninth century.

The church, the monastery, and the entire Armenian village of Akhury, were all destroyed on June 20, 1840 when an earthquake shook the mountain and swept everything away. The site has not been rebuilt. Indeed, the earthquake so thoroughly buried the village and monastery, that later travelers have not been able to locate any ruins from the site.

For the best photography, of Mt. Ararat, travel to Dogubeyazit, and journey just past town on the road toward the Iran border. This roadway follows the plain of Ararat, and offers views of both peaks of the mountain. The peaks are frequently obscured by clouds. The clearest weather, and the time when your chances of seeing both peaks is greatest, is in the spring.

To get there, first travel to either Van or Kars. From each of these cities there are regularly scheduled buses and mini-vans to Dogubeyazit. The town of Dogubeyazit is the point from which most expeditions to Ararat are begun.

GETTING TO KARS

There are several flights to Kars each day from Istanbul and Ankara. The most convenient way to travel directly to Kars from the US or Canada is by flying first to Istanbul, and then connecting on a Turkish Airlines flight from Istanbul to Kars. The Kars airport is about four kilometers outside the city.

The Kars bus station, the *otogar*, is just outside the city limits. There is a free shuttle that takes you from the bus station to the city center.

There's no mass transportation to Ani. Instead, plan to travel first to Kars, and then travel to Ani by taxi, or by shared hotel van. Expect to pay about 120 Turkish Lira (about US$60) for a round trip taxi from Kars to Ani, which includes the cost of having the driver wait for you at Ani for about three hours.

When to Visit

Kars is one of the coldest regions of historic Armenia and is apt to have snow on the ground as late as April and as early as November. Wait until after May for the most comfortable conditions. Hikers interested in scaling Mt. Ararat should plan to limit their travels to the month of August.

Suggested Itinerary

This suggested itinerary covers the highlights of the Kars region, in roughly the order of significance of the sites.

1. Day One: Early morning at Ani. Remain at Ani for at least three hours. Afternoon at the Fortress of Kars and at the Church of the Holy Apostles.

2. Day Two: South of Ani to the Monastery of Khtzkonk (Five Churches) and then farther south to Mren. Late afternoon just north of Ani at Horomos.

3. Day Three: View Mt. Ararat from Dogubeyazit while en route to Van.

The Monastery of Soorp Tovmas near the southern shore of Lake Van

Van

LAKE VAN

Apahunik

Panon (Pani)
*Kenaber
ARJĒSH (ERCHISH)
Hargin
Sinamēsh
Aghiovit
Muja (Mucha)
(Yukari Pete)
Kantsag (Kenzek)
Antsav (Anzav)
Ōroran (Orane)
Kratskar (Kadirasker)
Dēri Chai
*S. T'at'os
PERKRI
(Dergezin)
(Komaoso)
Ardzonivank'/
Jenaporivank'/
Akserva (Aksaraf)
Erikawpert?
(Ashaghi Arnis)
Argelan
Bzdig-kiugh
Eghavank' (Kizilkilise)
(Akkilise)
(Arnis)
(Küchük-köy)
S. T'at'os
S Spahan (Süphan)
P'esnakomer
Aghsraf
Plurmag / Belur-Manik (Plur)
(Karahan)
(Arestawan)?
Aregh (Üte)
(Binjevan)
P'eshne-Sur
Madghavank'
Madghavank'
(Arestawan)?
Antsav (Anzaf)
(Peshnekkömür)
Norshēn (Norshin)
(Medavank')
(Cape Medavank')
(Panz)
(Shivekār)
K'eoshk (Köshk)
Nakhavkavank'
Sip'an (Sübhan)
(Esheksorik)
Arberani
(Avkars)
Kordzut' Gortsot'
(4434 / 14547)
(Cape Eskiköy)
Limavank'
Dirashēn
(Körzot)
(Ashaghi Derjement)
(Jihangir)
Garak'eshish
S. K'ristapor
Khluvank'
Kusat'an
(Karakeshish)
Khzhishk*
(Ikinji)
(Mezraa)
(Hajiali)
(2700 / 8858)
Van
Norshēn (Nurshin)
(Kushen)
Orangachi (Örenkadi)
Amiugupert
Amiug
Chanig Matur (Manik)
(Kebabik)
Sat'ibeg (Seydibe)
Kefkale
Skaneh'elakortz' /
Diravank'
Kusat'an Atēr (Adir)
Urmm
(Kusku)
Metsnunik'
(Velijani)
Hrashakortz
(Tiravank
Arjra Nerk'in
Chakhmak (Chakmak)
"Monestery of Miracles"
yayla)
(Ashaghi Akjira?)
Novovans (Norvanis)
(Pirsulan)
(Sarimehmet)
(Aklaji)
(Manik)
L. Aygir
Artzravank'
Arjrn Vorin
Shahkealti (Shahgeldi)
Merganchugh
(Yukari Akjira)
(Meydanik)
Ardeviz
Haskündürük
Khorants
Aren (Arin)
Ērerin (Iririn)
Der Bedovank'
Pir-garir (Pirgarin)
Chermug (Chermik)
(Pathos)
Khorants
Arnchgoys
S. Sahak / Ērernavank'
Sosrat' (Susurat)
Hashp'shad (Ashagi Esbishat)
Tk'uts'vank'
(Horans)
(Arinökūs)
Bazents' (Panzis)
Koms (Kom)*
Adiljevaz
Gozokh
Koghus
Fargat / Pargat'
Ēchmiatznivank'*
K'eochani (Köchni)
(Pakis)
Gozokh
(Perkat)
Kocheni)*
Uri / Ori (Uri)
Drakpor
Ayants' (Ayans)
Keolu
Atēr / Hidir (Adir)
Goj (Koch)
Awervank'
Aliur (Alai)
(Göllū)
Adigüzel
LAKE
Shihayna
Satibey
ARJISHAG
Arjishak
(Mollakasim)
Bayrek)
Kiusnents
(Hireshik)
Arjishag /
Anavank'
Kōprū köy)
(Kasimoghlu)
Archag (Erchek)
Anavank'
Ktuts Island
Bogunik'
Payunik
Kōlsatan
Ghezl-cha (Kozluja)
(Gürdivan)
Marmet
(Zihter)
Mermenid / Almashad
Napat' (Nabat)
(Aktash)
Monastery of Ktuts
Zeve (Ekmal)
Boghants'
(Poghanis)
Baliki
(Bardakji)
Everek
(Adiyaman)
2890 / 9482
Sevan (Seivan)
Major Urartian site
(Kaleik)
L. Ermanis
Farugh (Faruk)
Sewakrag (Seivan kale)
Zarants' (Zeranis)
Awants'
Lēzk'
(Shahbaghi)
Ermants' (Ermanis)
(Iskeleköy)
Toprakkale
Eskipak
(Hasamiyan)
Van Kale
[Toprakkale]
Kokhpants'
(Sihke)
Zirvandanis
(Lamizgert)
(Kisran)
VAN
Tosp
(Kōsh kōy)
Shushants' (Shushanis)
Shushants'
Varag
Upper Varag
Varakavank'
3194 /10479
L. Varag
Varak
Toni (Doni)
(Yedikilise)
ARDAMED (ADREMID)
(Keshishoghlu)
Katepants'
Dzvsdan (Zivistan)
S. Vartan of Aregh
K'runkvank'
Pertag (Pertek)
Aregh (Arikan)
Artashesean
Norkiugh
Hayots Tsor
Aghnakants'
P'egants' / Yikanes (Pinganis)
(Norgūh)
S. Kevork of Koms
S. Vartan (Suvartan)
Artawanean?
Lēzk' (Han)
S. Yarut'yun
Khndrakatarivank'
S. Gevorg
Hntstan (Hindistan)
Koms / Akom
(Ahnatap cove)
Ishkhanikom
Mashdag
Srkhuvank'
(Naniki)
(Haykaberd)
Khoshap
(Komus)
(Devebuynu Peninsula)
Kawavnank'
(Maskatak)
Aprahami V.
Tsitsaghaberivank'
(Hoshap)
[Hoghts]
(Cape Ahnatap)
Artsuaperivank'
S. Vartan
Ankgh
Gēm
(Kigzi)
(Iremit)
Ordok' (Ōrtūk)
Oghvants'
Ngaravank'
(Cape Morno)
Khorkom
Karavans
Kaipalasan
Bezhngerd
Oghvants'
Haghun
In Bay
Miulk' (Mūlk)
(Gelberhasan)
(Mijingir)
Verin Bzhngerd
(Haji kōy)
(Mrors
Egheghis (Göllū)
Aghin (Agin)
Inkōy
Khorakants' V.
Gogants'
(Mijingir-Ulia)
K'rel (Kiril)
S. Tovma of Mrors
Vafents (Varis)
Arter Island
Kharagants
Mards
Khumsayank'
Zev
S Astvatsatsin
(Haire-Kianis)
Mollahüseyin)
Gentrans
Bagh
Sakhuravank' (Pelli)
Aghtamar Island
Kiziltash
K'erts'
Khosp
Dimkosin
(Asras)
Garmragvank'
(Herch
(Hosp)
Arants'
Shadvan (Satvan)
Soorp Khatch
Hirj)
Pagakeatug (Pagagedik)
3060 / 10039
(Pindivanis)
Erewark
S. Tovma
Khntsorgen (Kinasor)
Kom
(Gürūndū)
Mokhrapert (Muhrabit)
Manakert
Pellu (Pelli)
Norkiugh
(Iskirt)
Karatasho (Kiretash)
S Yagop of Nisibis
(Norkūh)
Sare-Verin (Sarik)
Atanan
(Pürūz)
P'shavants'
(V)OSTAN (GEVASH)
(Pishvanis)
Engeler)
Nareg (Narik)
Pertatsorivank'
Rshtunik'
Iluvank (Ilivanik)
S. Nshan Chārahan
Khrordents /
Mulk
Horevit
3475 /11401
Chavushtepe
Hurudis (Hürūhtūs)
Haght (Aht)
Dshogh (Dūshuk)
[Sardurihinili]
Ganchars (Kanjas)
Pahvanis)
(Salis)
Poghonis
(Irichvanik)
(Poghanis)
3750 / 12303
(Ahkis)
(Varis)
Horodis)
Harpert (Arpit)
Shahurapert
Pashat (Beshet)

Courtesy of Robert H. Hewsen

Elevation

9,000 + ft

7,000 ft

5,000 ft

3,000 ft

◉ Province Capital

◉ District Center

(Yedikilise) Turkish Name

◆ Monastery

♁ Church / Chapel

■ Fortress

□ Ruined Fortress

— Road

• Armenian Village

Scale

0 .... 6 km.

0 ... 2 ... 4 ... 6 mi.

Van

INTRODUCTION

Van is the heartland of historic Armenia. The region of Van and the ancient **Kingdom of Vaspurakan** is paired with the plains of Ararat as the cradles of Armenian civilization.

For hundreds of years, and continuing through the beginning of the twentieth century, the population of Armenians here often exceeded that of any other national group. Throughout the millennia these Armenians have contributed greatly to the political and cultural development of the Armenian nation.

The architectural relics of many of these contributions are still present in the region today. Indeed, they are present here in far greater numbers than in most other parts of historic Armenia. This multitude of sites is certainly one of the reasons that Van is a leading destination for pilgrims who are searching for their roots in the lost Armenian homeland—there's just so much to see in this one region.

Despite this wealth of Armenian history, Van, and the rest of the historic Armenian homeland in present-day Turkey, has been largely ignored by pilgrims and by other visitors for most of the past century.

For decades, tourism to the historically Armenian areas of eastern Turkey, and particularly to the area around Van, was restricted. Turkey had declared the area to be a military zone, and traveling there was either subject to red tape and mandatory escorts, or it wasn't allowed at all.

Turkey imposed travel restrictions partly because the region sits along the sensitive borders of Syria and Iraq. For most of the twentieth century, eastern Turkey also shared a long frontier with the Soviet Union—a front line for the Cold War. Foreign visitors weren't welcome.

The demography of Van and of eastern Turkey also discouraged some travelers. After the elimination of the Armenians from historic Armenia, the surviving population of eastern Turkey was almost entirely Kurdish. A Kurdish separatist movement kept the region restive and inhospitable to all but the heartiest of travelers.

Today, however, the region is calm, military restrictions have been lifted, and Turkey has tentatively begun to encourage tourism to Van and to the entire Lake Van region. One century after the Armenian Genocide, a new generation of ethnic Armenians has, equally tentatively, begun to rediscover its lost homeland.

The restoration and repair of Aghtamar a few years ago appears to be part of this effort to vitalize tourism in Van. The repairs were controversial but they appear to have been part of a successful effort to attract more visitors.

Hearty travelers who are willing to venture beyond Aghtamar will find that the Armenia of their imagination is still here, hidden in the foothills of obscurity, waiting to be rediscovered.

The Island of Aghtamar

HIGHLIGHTS OF VAN

Perhaps the most famous and most visited Armenian site at Van, and within the entire lost Armenian homeland, is **Soorp Khatch** (the **Cathedral of the Holy Cross**) on the island of **Aghtamar**. This tenth century cathedral was once part of a sprawling monastic compound, and a center of the Armenian Apostolic Church. This beautifully sited monument sits on a small island near the southeastern shore of Lake Van.

The Cathedral was seized by Turkey in 1915, but each year in September, since 2010, Armenians from around the world travel to Aghtamar to participate in the divine liturgy of the Armenian Church. The liturgy, which is known to Armenians as the *badarak*, is an elaborate and formal church service, and evokes the cultural memory of the Armenians of Van.

Apart from Aghtamar, the ruins of the Armenian town of **Old Van** are the highlight of any visit to this region. Old Van was destroyed one hundred years ago, but its pathways and foundations are still evident today at the base of the **Rock of Van**. This old Armenian Van is located about three kilometers west of the newly built city of Van.

Varagavank, which is known locally as **Yedi Kilise**, is located a few kilometers outside the city of Van, and is on the short-list of must-see sites in Van. This once spectacular monastery today engenders both heartbreak and hope.

The *heartbreak* of Varagavank is its senseless destruction and the subsequent misuse of its ruins, for many decades, as a stable and barn. The *hope* of Varagavank, however, arises from its modest renovation and its fitful use in recent years as an Armenian church.

Most of Varagavank was destroyed by the Turkish Army in 1915, but the small remnant that survived is today maintained by Armenians under the patronage of the Armenian Patriarch of Istanbul. The site is watched by a caretaker who lives in the Kurdish village that sprouted there following the destruction of the monastery.

During the decades following the destruction of Varagavank, throughout the twentieth century, Turkey continued to destroy, actively or passively, most of the architectural evidence of the three thousand year-old Armenian civilization in Van and throughout historic Armenia.

Sites that weren't bombed or dismantled were allowed to fall into disrepair, sometimes irreparably. Aghtamar had at one point been scheduled for destruction, too, but earned a last minute reprieve in 1951 after a prominent Kurd from the region intervened.

By 2007, Turkey appeared to signal that it might be changing its approach to the stewardship of Armenian cultural sites, however. The government took the unprecedented step of renovating Aghtamar, and of converting the sacred site to a state museum. By the end of 2014, a sign had been erected that, for the first time in a century, identified Aghtamar as an Armenian church.

The renovation was not without controversy. And the conversion of an Armenian church to a state-owned secular museum is not endorsed by Armenians. But the move did give rise to hope—regardless of Turkey's motivation—that the surviving ancient Armenian churches of historic Armenia would not be targeted for destruction.

Van, as the heartland of the Armenian nation, had an abundance of churches and monasteries in 1915. Because of their sheer number, it seems that after 100 years more of them have survived here than anywhere else in modern-day Turkey.

This makes the entire region of Van—not just the city and its environs—a fertile ground for explorers who are seeking the sites of the lost Armenian homeland. Incidentally, visiting these sites might also have the effect of encouraging their current custodians to follow the lead taken at Aghtamar, and to preserve, rather than destroy, the sites that are still standing.

A BRIEF HISTORY OF VAN

The history of the Armenians in Van dates back to the origin of the Armenia nation, to the time of **Hayk**, the legendary father of the Armenians. This history continued through the centuries, until 1915.

According to legend, Hayk had established a fortress in **Hayots Dzor**—the **Valley of the Armenians**—and this region had become known as **Hayastan**. Hayots Dzor was located on the Armenian Plateau in the region of Van—an area that was also known by the alternative geographic term, the Armenian Highland.

By the ninth century BC, an Urartian kingdom of Van had been founded by the Armenian leader Aram, and history records that there was an Armenian city of Van in 550 BC.

Historical accounts also show an Armenian kingdom of Van in the fourth century AD. The name Vaspurakan appeared shortly thereafter as the name of a vast province that united some 35 disparate districts.

The famous Armenian **Kingdom of Vaspurakan** with which most students of Armenian history are familiar was formed in AD 908 and survived for roughly one century, until AD 1021. Scholars acclaim **King Gagik** as the greatest of the Kings of Vaspurakan.

During his reign, which lasted from 908 until 943, King Gagik erected many secular and religious buildings, built an aqueduct from the summit of Mt. Varag, to nearby Van, and constructed the Cathedral of the Holy Cross at Aghtamar. The thousand-year-old monastery of Narek, which was located just west of the town of Van until its destruction by Turkey in 1915, was also founded during King Gagik's reign.

The capital of the Kingdom of Vaspurakan was for a time sited at Van, but the capital had no fixed seat, and the king moved about as he saw fit. King Gagik chose the island of Aghtamar as his residence, and hence as the capital of Vaspurakan, during his reign. Aghtamar is closely affiliated with Van, and it is geographically close, as well. As a result, the common misperception that Van was *always* the capital of Vaspurakan, and that it was the *only* capital, is one that is easy to overlook.

Beginning in the eleventh century, the Kingdom of Vaspurakan fell under the dominion of a succession of invaders starting with Seljuk Turks and Mongols, and continuing with Turkmen and Kurdish notables. By the sixteenth century, Vaspurakan was conquered by the Ottomans. These lands that were once ruled by King Gagik, and which remained populated with a plurality of Armenians, were ultimately incorporated into the Ottoman Empire as the *vilayet*, or province, of Van.

Throughout all these centuries of occupation, the Armenian community of Van, and elsewhere in Armenia, maintained its cohesiveness through religion, rather than politics, and through sectarian, rather than secular, leaders. The greatest Armenian authority for most of this period was the **Catholicosate of Aghtamar**, which had its headquarters on the island of Aghtamar.

By the late 1800s, the prestige of Aghtamar had declined, however, and by 1895 it had become vacant. Aghtamar would never recover. The island was pillaged by Kurds in 1915.

Its status as a See of the Armenian Church was dissolved the following year when Turkey seized all of the church properties on the island, including the Cathedral of the Holy Cross, following the genocide.

During these years of tumult, the monastery of Varagavank, under the leadership of Mkrtich Khrimian—a priest who would later become affectionately known as **Khrimian Hayrig** (Father Khrimian)—assumed the leadership of the Armenian community of Van.

But Varagavank, too, would perish. The Turkish Army destroyed the monastery in April 1915, during its military campaign against the Armenians of the town of Van.

In 1915, and continuing through early 1918, many of the Armenians from Van who survived the genocide fled east across the border to Yerevan, which was then a small town in the region known as Russian Armenia. Other survivors fled south, seeking refuge in Syria and Iraq.

During the final exodus from Van in April 1918, approximately 25,000 Armenians fled to Persia. With this last exodus, a continuous 2,500-year presence of Armenians in Van had come to an end. Van, which had been one of the six Armenian provinces (*vilayets*) of the Ottoman Empire, was no longer home to any Armenians.

Population

According to the census data of the Armenian Patriarchate, the Armenians of Van formed an absolute majority of the population in 1912. This majority existed in the *sanjak*, or district, of Van, which included places such as Van, Aygestan, and Varagavank, all along the southern shore of Lake Van.

This census counted the population of Van as consisting of 185,000 Armenians, 47,000 Turks, 40,000 Nomadic Kurds, and 32,000 Sedentary Kurds. There were also smaller populations of Assyrians, Yezidis, and Gypsies. The total population was recorded as 350,000. Thus, the Armenians held an absolute majority, at least according to the census of the Armenian Patriarchate.

Population tallies by others, including by the Turkish authorities, generally showed fewer Armenians and more Turks and Kurds.

Armenians were not a majority of the population in the vast *vilayet* of Van, however. Armenians lost their majority status in the late 1800s when the Ottoman government merged the Armenian *vilayet* of Van with the heavily populated Kurdish *sanjak* of Hakkari. The town of Hakkari, from which the Hakkari *sanjak* takes its name, is about 200 kilometers southeast of Van, on the Iraq frontier.

The result of this merger was a super-sized *vilayet* of roughly 47,700 square kilometers in which the Armenian population

had become diluted by the addition of large numbers of Kurds. The motivation for the border manipulation, say scholars, was to reduce the political influence of Armenians and other non-Muslim minorities.

Regardless of the exact population tallies, it is unchallenged that the Armenians constituted a significant part of the population of Van until 1915. The old walled city of Van had a population of about 3,750 in 1915, of whom two thirds were Armenian and the rest Turks. By 2010, the population of the municipality of Van alone was 367,419 according to the official census. This most-recent census figure reports no Armenians among the population.

A detailed analysis of the demography of Van province during the years 1844 through 1914 was compiled by Armenia scholar Sarkis Y. Karayan and is published in *Armenian Van – Vaspurakan*, the first volume in the UCLA Armenian History and Culture Series.

Van and Paradise

Through the ages, when the Armenians of Van talked lovingly about their home, they were apt to quote the proverb: Van in this world and paradise in the next.

After the British subject **H. F. B. Lynch** returned from his travels throughout Armenia in the 1890s, he struggled to reconcile this Armenian proverb with the realities of life that he observed among the Armenians of Van.

He wrote in his epic tome *Armenia: Travels and Studies* that the proverb was no longer appropriate. The comparison might have been justified under happier circumstances, Lynch wrote, but the perversity of man had converted this heaven into a little hell.

Upon further consideration, however, Lynch recanted. Despite the sufferings of the Armenians, he concluded that Van's beautiful geography and its intriguing churches from antiquity "abundantly justify the Armenian proverb."

Van in 1915

Van is celebrated by Armenians today not only for the contributions of its residents to *ancient* Armenian history, but also for the bold resistance of the people of Van during the Armenian Genocide in 1915. This resistance was centered in the old walled city of Van, which is sometimes today called Old Van, and also in **Aygestan**, the so called "Garden District" that was located adjacent to the old city.

The Armenian defense at Van was an exception to the deportations and slaughter of the Armenian population in much of the rest of historic Armenia.

Robert H. Hewsen, the professor of history and Armenia scholar, describes what unfolded: "Marked for extermination in 1915, the Armenians of Van got wind of what was coming and armed themselves for a spirited self-defense. For almost a month, from April 20 until May 16, a few hundred men defended themselves and their loved ones, some 30,000 people, against a Turkish armed force."

The Armenians fortified themselves within the walled city of Van and in adjacent Aygestan, and hunkered down. As days passed, and then weeks, food and critical supplies became exhausted. The Turkish siege was on the verge of success. Support finally arrived from an advancing Russian army. The Armenians prevailed, briefly, and they established a provisional government, a **Republic of Van**.

For reasons that still puzzle modern historians, however, the Russians retreated from Van a few weeks later, causing the Armenians to flee, as well. The Russian army then recaptured Van later that year, and held it until April 1918, when—preoccupied with revolution in the Russian homeland—the Russians and the remaining Armenians made their final retreat.

Onnig Mukhitarian, a participant in the defense of Van, estimated at the time that the resistance of the Armenians of Van had saved the lives of 200,000 civilians. He identifies **Vahan** and **Mihran Kheranian** as two of the leaders of the defense of Van.

THE DEFENSE OF VAN

The self-defense of the civilian Armenian population of Van in 1915 was one of only two successful efforts by Armenians to defend themselves during the Turkish genocide of the Armenians. The other successful defense was at **Musa Dagh**, which is located far to the west, near the shores of the Mediterranean Sea in the historically Armenian region of Kilikia (Giligia).

These defenses are considered successful because innocent lives were saved, and not because the Armenians ultimately prevailed in battle (they didn't). The civilian populations at Van and at Musa Dagh were both able to withstand sieges and then flee to safety.

The events at Van are memorialized in the book *The Defense of Van*, which is an eyewitness account of the struggle in 1915 to defend the city against the Turkish siege and bombardment. The book is written in two parts by authors Onnig Mukhitarian and Haig Gossoian. The struggle at Musa Dagh is famously depicted in the classic novel *The Forty Days of Musa Dagh*, by German author Franz Werfel.

Other notable Armenian efforts to resist the genocide occurred at **Urfa**, and at **Shabin-Karahisar**. The efforts here did not succeed, however, and the Armenian populations of each town were slaughtered.

Most Armenians in the Ottoman Empire did not resort to self-defense in 1915 because they initially accepted government assurances that they were merely being relocated, or, even when doubtful about these assurances, they did not understand the extent to which their lives were genuinely at risk.

Revisionist historians today characterize the self-defense of the Armenians at Van as an uprising that somehow justified the massacres and deportations that were perpetrated against Armenians throughout the entire empire.

Contemporaneous accounts by observers such as US Ambassador **Henry Morgenthau** show that the revisionist history is wrong. The actions of the Armenians of Van were a response to, rather than a provocation of, the massacres and deportations throughout the empire.

The Castle of Van
as it appeared in 1997, before reconstruction

VISITING VAN TODAY

There are three compelling sites of interest to Armenian pilgrims within the municipality of Van: The **Rock of Van**, which is known locally as **Van Kalesi**, the **Van Museum**, which is located in the new city of Van, and the Armenian town of **Old Van**.

Old Van today lies in ruins at the base of the Rock of Van, about three kilometers west of the new city. The town was destroyed about 100 years ago and has been abandoned and unpopulated ever since. Old Van, and the adjacent district of Aygestan, are the famous sites where the civilian Armenian population in 1915 took up arms in self-defense against the Ottoman Turkish Army.

The Rock of Van is no longer used as a citadel, but it has been reconstructed in recent years. The restoration facilitates tourism, rather than national defense. Visit both the ghost town of Old Van and the Rock together.

For the best photography, plan your visit to Old Van so that you arrive in early morning, just after sunrise. Enter through the ruins of the town, which is not gated and has no entry fee. The lighting in early morning will allow you to make photographs from a vantage point that includes the Rock, the ruins, and the lake.

Construction of the new city of Van, which is about three kilometers from Old Van, began in the 1920s. The population of this new city is almost entirely Kurdish. Armenians have never lived in the new city, except for the hidden Armenians of historic Armenia.

Old Van, c. 1915
Photo from C.F. Lehmann-Haupt, Armenien einst und jetzt (Berlin/Leipzig, 1926)

Old Van, 2014

The Rock of Van

The Rock of Van, also known as Van Kalesi or Van Castle, is the most striking geographic feature of Van. This great rock is more than one kilometer long, and more than 100 meters tall. The south side of the rock abuts the town of Old Van, and is a sheer vertical cliff from its base to the summit.

After the Ottomans captured Van in the sixteenth century, a citadel was built atop the rock. The citadel was said to have become one of the most powerful fortresses of the Ottoman Empire. The British traveler H. F. B. Lynch compared its shape to the back of a camel, with the citadel occupying the hump. The fortress atop the Rock of Van has undergone significant renovations in recent years, and a reconstruction was still underway at time of research.

Old Van

The old Armenian town of **Van** sits at the southern base of the Rock of Van. The town was heavily damaged in 1915 during the siege of Van and during its bombardment by the Turkish Army. The rest of the town was burned and completely destroyed in 1918.

The appearance of the town has not changed much since 1918. Some of the Armenian ruins have deteriorated further, and a pair of mosques has undergone extensive renovation and reconstruction during the past twenty years. Apart from the rebuilding of the two mosques, there has been no attempt to reconstruct or to revitalize the area.

The appearance of the *terrain* has undergone a modest change over the years, however. After the town was destroyed, treasure hunters descended upon the ruins, as they did elsewhere in historic Armenia, seeking the gold and jewelry that they believed the Armenians had hidden beneath the foundations of their homes and churches.

Over the years, the holes that they dug became partly back-filled with soil. This accounts for the undulating appearance of some of the landscape.

From the vantage at the top of the Rock of Van, one can imagine the flurry of activity that must have accompanied life in the town below. From this vantage, as well, one can more easily discern the streets and pathways of Old Van. At ground level, the flattened city appears to be barely more than a large field, interrupted only by the pair of newly restored mosques and a scattering of Armenian ruins.

Prior to its destruction, Old Van had been a densely populated and walled city, with separate quarters for its Muslim and Armenian populations. The **Armenian Quarter** dominated, and covered about 75 percent of the area of the town. Many of the buildings were just one story tall, giving the city a squat and low-lying profile. Old Van was fortified with a double line of walls and a moat, and access was gained through four gates.

In 1909, less than a decade before its destruction, there had been seven Armenian churches within the city walls of Old Van, grouped mostly at the center of town, and near the base of the rock.

The ruins of the **Hisopian School for Boys**, and of the **Soorp Vartan Church**, are the most prominent Armenian ruins that are present today. They are both located near the base of the rock at the northeastern part of town. A century ago, this part of town was the heart of the Armenian district. At time of research, there were no plans to restore any of the Armenian ruins.

To get there, from the center of the new city of Van, travel roughly three kilometers west of the city, on the road that is signposted for Van Kalesi. This road takes you along the north side of the Rock of Van. At the end of the road there is a gated entrance (with a small entry fee) to the Rock.

From this entrance you can either walk up the steps to the top of the Rock, or walk around to the south side of the Rock to the ruins of Old Van. You can also walk to the ruins of Old Van from the south side of the Rock. Allow one half day to fully explore both Old Van and the citadel atop the Rock of Van.

The gate to Old Van and the Rock of Van, c. 1915
Photo by Vartan A. Hampikian, Courtesy of John Donelian

The ruins of Old Van, 1997

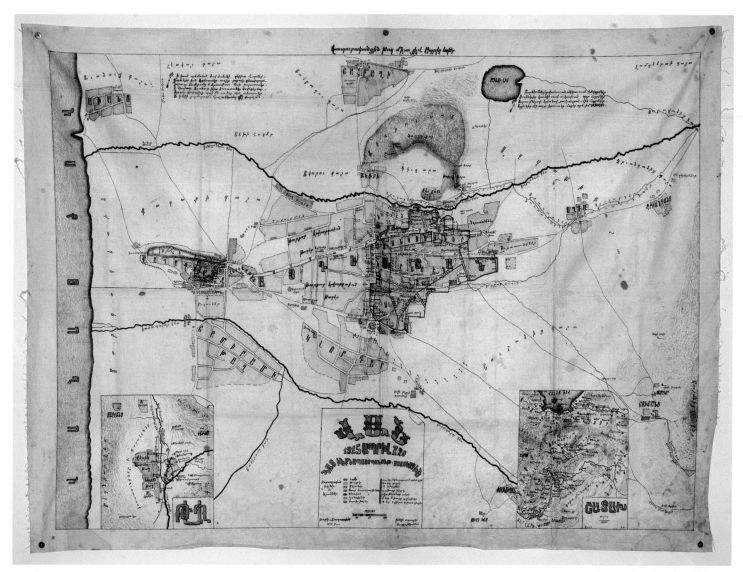

Map of the Defense of Van by Mardiros Kheranian

MAPPING THE DEFENSE OF VAN

Mardiros Kheranian was a professional cartographer who had lived in Van during its siege by Ottoman Turkey. He also taught at the Monastery of Varagavank and participated in the defense of Van in 1915.

In 1927, nearly a decade after Van had burned to the ground and after he and the rest of Van's Armenians had become refugees, Kheranian created the map that appears on the facing page.

The Armenian letters at the bottom center of the map spell the word "Van." The inscription "1915 [April] 7/20" refers to the date of the start of the siege of Van. The Turks began their siege of Van on April 20, 1915, but since the USSR was still using the old Julian calendar at the time the map was created, Kheranian used the Julian date of April 7, as well.

The text that appears below the date identifies the drawing as a chart of the self-defense of Van. Kheranian shows the locations of the Armenian fighters, their lines of defense, and the locations of Turkish and Armenian guards. The map is thus a priceless historical record of the defense of Van, as well as a work of art. The poetic text in the upper corners of the map describe Van's beauty before the siege, and its devastation afterward.

Kheranian drew this map by hand, using ink on cloth. The original measures 37 x 56 inches (95 x 142 cm) and is on display at Armenia's **National Museum** in Yerevan. Kheranian also created the map of historic Armenia that appears on the inside back cover. That map shows Armenia as it appeared in 1915, and measures 42 x 66 inches (107 x 166 cm). Kheranian's family in the US owns the original.

Mardiros Kheranian was part of a large family of Kheranians who had lived in Van in 1915. The 1930 publication The Defense of Van, which was written by an eyewitness to the siege, identifies **Mihran Khranian (Kheranian)** as the leader of two defense posts, and **Khatchig** and **Vahan Khranian (Kheranian)** as combatants. Family member **Yeghishe Kheranian** was a Vardabed (High Priest) at Karmravor. The writer **Mkrtich Kheranian** was also a *Vanetsi* (native of Van) from this family. Author **Matthew Karanian** is a descendant of this family.

Aygestan

Aygestan played a significant part in the history of Old Van. This was the so-called Orchard or Garden District of Van, which some have characterized as Van's wealthy suburb.

Aygestan was adjacent to Van, and filled a district of eight square miles just southeast of the city, but this is probably where the city-suburb comparison ends. H. F. B. Lynch characterized the relationship between Aygestan and Van as similar to the relationship between London's West End and the City of London. Thus, one can imagine that Aygestan and Van enjoyed a complementary status, and that their populations were mutually dependent.

The wealthier classes were drawn to Aygestan because of its open spaces, its wide tree-lined streets, and all the fresh air. Van, by contrast, was crowded and compact. The relative comfort of Aygestan made this district the setting of choice for foreign consulates and missions, as well.

The American Congregationalist mission was located here, and was important to the civic life of the Armenians until 1915. Its compound included a church, hospital, several schools open to both boys and girls, and four large residential buildings. Apart from the church of this mission, Aygestan district was home to five Armenian churches.

Van Museum

The building that houses the **Van Museum** was closed for repairs following the earthquake that struck Van in 2011. The municipality plans to build a new museum near the Fortress. Until then, there are numerous artifacts, including Urartian monuments, which are available for viewing in the outdoor yard of the old museum.

If the museum is open at the time of your visit, go with a sense of wonder, but don't expect accuracy in the historical displays. The museum gained notoriety when it displayed an anti-Armenian exhibit that purported to prove that Christian Armenians had committed genocide in 1915 against Van's Muslim population.

That exhibit was removed in 2008, leaving the museum completely silent about the history of Armenians in Van. The old museum is located at the eastern end of the city of Van, on Kisla Street (Kisla Caddesi).

Arshile Gorky

The brilliant abstract expressionist painter **Arshile Gorky** was born Vosdanig Adoian sometime around 1902 or 1904 in the village of Khorkom, near Lake Van. He was not more than 13 years old in 1915 when he witnessed the massacres and ethnic cleansing of the Armenians of Van.

In the summer of 1915 he was able to escape Van and flee eastward with his mother across the Ottoman-Russian frontier to Yerevan.

He was still a teenager in 1918 when he and his mother, Shushan, attempted to flee the deprivations and the specter of death in the refugee city of Yerevan by walking to Tbilisi, a distance of about 270 kilometers.

They never made it. Shushan was malnourished and too weak for the walk. She died of starvation just outside Yerevan the following year.

By 1920 Gorky was finally able to immigrate to the US. This is when he changed his name to Arshile Gorky, in honor of the famous Russian writer Maxim Gorky.

Back in 1912, before the genocide and while he was still in Van, Gorky had posed for a photograph with his mother. This is the photograph that would later inspire Gorky to create the renowned painting **The Artist and His Mother**.

After making it to the US, Gorky lived briefly in Watertown, Massachusetts, and then in New York City, and finally in the small town of Sherman, Connecticut. He committed suicide on July 21, 1948, at his home in Sherman. He is buried at a cemetery next to a church in town.

JUST OUTSIDE VAN

Varagavank was founded early in the eleventh century and eventually became reputed to be the richest monastery in the region. The monastic complex formed a spectacular and stately presence on the foothills of Mt. Varag, just eight kilometers east of the city of Van, until its destruction by the Turkish Army in April 1915.

The site is known locally by its Turkish name, **Yedi Kilise**, which means Seven Churches. Of course there are no longer seven churches here, but the name persists. After the loss of the monastery, a Kurdish village sprouted on the site. The name of this village is Bakracli, but there are many who refer to the village as Yedi Kilise. If you tell someone in Van that you want to travel to Yedi Kilise, they'll know exactly where you want to go.

The Armenian King Senekerim-Hovhannes of Vaspurakan is credited with having founded the monastery as early as AD 1003. The seventeenth and eighteenth centuries were said to be a golden age for Varagavank, but the nineteenth century wasn't as kind. Varagavank came under frequent raids by Kurdish tribes, and in 1896 the monastery was sacked.

Throughout the centuries, the most precious treasure to be housed at Varagavank was probably a fragment of the cross upon which Jesus was crucified. This relic is fabled to have been originally brought to this site by two Armenian saints back in the third century, long before the monastery was even founded.

The cross was then lost on the mountain for a few hundred years, and then found again in the seventh century. During all these centuries, the fragment of the cross was apparently always on Mt. Varag. And so when Varagavank was built in the eleventh century, it made sense to just keep it there.

The fragment was finally packed up and was moved to Sebastia in AD 1021, which is the year that the King of Vaspurakan ceded his kingdom to the Byzantine Empire in exchange for what he must have thought was a better deal farther west. After the king died,

the relic found its way back to Varagavank, and then ultimately to the church of Soorp Nishan in the walled city of Van. The cross was stored in this church during the siege of Van in 1915, and it is presumed to have been destroyed.

Varagavank was for many years the seat of the Archbishop of the Armenian Church, and by the late nineteenth century it had supplanted Aghtamar as the religious center for the Armenians of Van. The monastery was home to historic Armenia's first printing press.

The charismatic priest Mkrtich Khrimian published historic Armenia's first newspaper—**The Eagle of Vaspurakan**—here in 1858. This priest would later become the leader of the Armenian Church, and would become known as **Khrimian Hayrig**.

The destruction of Varagavank in 1915 was apparently a strategic move by the Turkish Army. The monastery had been a center of the Armenian community. When the Turkish Army captured the site on April 25, 1915, the Armenians were deprived of using Varagavank as a refuge, or as a place for retreat from Van.

Actually, at the time of its capture, Varagavank was *already* filled with Armenian refugees from the deportations and massacres. Some 5,000 of these refugees then fled to Aygestan, which placed a further burden on the resources of the Armenians there. The Turkish Army destroyed the monastery five days later, on April 30, 1915.

To get there, hire a taxi from the city of Van, because there is no regular public transportation to Varagavank. The distance is only about eight kilometers, and a round trip taxi, including one hour of waiting time, should cost about $20. Negotiate the fare in advance. The monastery is usually locked but the custodian has the key and will open it for visitors. There is no fee for this. Some visitors choose to purchase a candle or two from the custodian and light it in the church. **GPS map coordinates** for Varagavank: 38 27' 0" N, 43 27' 41" E

Varagavank, c. 1914
Photo by Vartan A. Hampikian, Courtesy of John Donelian

Varagavank, 2003

Varagavank, 2014

On April 30, 1915, the Turkish Army bombed the monastery of Varagavank.
Its arches collapsed during an earthquake in 2011. Today, a Kurdish village
has developed in the area surrounding this once stately monastic compound.

Varagavank, 2014

Varagavank interior

THE EAGLE OF VASPURAKAN

Mkrtich Khrimian, the leader of the Armenian people who would later become fondly known as **Khrimian Hayrig**, founded the first newspaper ever printed in Armenia in 1858 while he was a young priest at Varagavank.

This newspaper, **Artsvi Vaspurakan (The Eagle of Vaspurakan)** helped Armenians to develop a national consciousness during the late 1800s. Mkrtich Khrimian would later become Catholicos (leader) of the Armenian Church.

Khrimian Hayrig was the moniker bestowed upon Mkrtich Khrimian by his flock out of admiration and fondness. Hayrig is the diminutive form of the word Hayr, which is the Armenian word for Father.

The Eagle of Vaspurakan is today honored with a monument in the Republic of Armenia. The monument, which depicts an eagle with its wings spread, sits atop a hill along the major highway that links Yerevan to Lake Sevan.

VARAGAVANK TODAY

When I first saw Varagavank in 2003, I did not immediately realize that I was at a sacred monastic site. The exterior of the surviving buildings resembled old stone barns. A blood red Turkish flag was hanging prominently on the wall of a church—the one church that had survived the assault upon the monastery a century earlier.

The interiors looked unlike churches, too. They were filled with hay, and with quarry materials, and with building supplies.

When I returned a decade later, in 2013, I saw that the three arches at the front of Soorp Astvatsatsin had collapsed during the Van earthquake of 2011. Their pillars were now prostrate on the ground, an addition to the ruins of the site.

But inside, I was surprised to see that the farm supplies were gone, and that an Armenian church had returned. The Armenian Patriarchate of Istanbul had provided financial support for a minor, but nevertheless significant, cleanup of the interior.

The church had an altar. And candles. And a cross.

To be sure, the interior was primitive, and had certainly not been restored to its magnificent condition of 1914. Indeed, there is no restoration at all. The hole in the roof where the dome and drum had once stood is still a hole in the roof.

Still, I was pleased to see that this church once again looks like a church. Local villagers had been receptive to this cleanup. They expected that they might earn some money from the tourists and pilgrims who would visit. According to a report in the US-based *Armenian Weekly* newspaper, however, the deed to the church, and to the other properties of the village, is held by an individual, the descendant of a prominent Turk from the region who somehow acquired title after 1915.

Prominently displayed on one of the pillars, someone—maybe the local caretaker—had posted a copy of an antique photograph of the monastery as it had appeared one hundred years ago. The photograph might have been intended as a memorial to encourage visitors to mourn the loss of Varagavank. But I viewed the photograph as a challenge to rebuild all that has been lost.

Narekavank, the Monastery of Narek, was constructed in the tenth century on the southern shoreline of Lake Van during the era of Grigor Narekatsi. Its location is just west of the boat launch for Aghtamar, which is in the modern town of Gevash. This majestic monastic complex was destroyed and leveled in 1915. There are no ruins or remnants to view their today.

The grave of Grigor Narekatsi may still be in the area, but I have not seen it and am not aware of any credible reports that the grave has been preserved. If you look for this grave, you will be searching amid a Kurdish village and a mosque that was built on the site during the past century.

Narekavank may be contemplated today only through the handful of antique photographs that survive from a century ago, and from the descriptions of experts who have studied the complex. Nairy Hampikian is one of those experts. She is a scholar of Armenian architecture and the author of many modern publications about the sites of historic Armenia.

Hampikian describes Narekavank as having been a fortified complex consisting of two churches, a meeting room and bell tower, the mausoleum of Narekatsi, and several administrative buildings and dwellings. According to Hampikian, the monastery of Narekavank "demonstrates how this and all other such complexes at one time dominated the landscape with their multiple pointed conical domes rising against the sky."

Edremit, located about 12 kilometers southwest of the city of Van, was until recently the site of a Medieval Armenian cemetery. The burial ground was extensive, and was situated on the slope of a hillside overlooking the town of Edremit. When I visited the site in 2013 I found apartment buildings on the hilltop, but none of the *khatchkars* (engraved stone crosses) that must have, until the modern era, filled the site.

Travelers who visited the site several years earlier reported that they observed rows of stone blocks at the site—stones that were not present in 2013. Each stone block had a rectangular cavity that served as the base for a vanished Armenian *khatchkar*. According to a report published by the Virtual Ani project, rows of these *khatchkar* bases "run along the highest point of the cemetery site and any *khatchkars* located there would have been visible from a great distance—perhaps from as far away as Van."

Edremit, which is a derivation of the old Armenian name Artemid, was once the site of a large Armenian village of about 350 homes. This village, which was also called Artemid, is now known by the Turkish name *Sarmansuyu*. In addition to being home to the plundered cemetery, the town is also the site of the botched renovation of its sole surviving Armenian artifact—an Armenian church.

This church did not have great architectural or historical significance apart from its status as the only surviving building of this Armenian village, but it was somehow targeted for renovation back in 2006. Instead of being properly renovated and restored, however, the structure was rebuilt in the appearance of a bunker, using a design that is alien to Armenian architecture.

The Virtual Ani project reports that the renovation is a politically inspired project that fundamentally altered the appearance of the church. The European Union's Eastern Anatolian Development Project funded the so-called restoration.

Visit this "renovated" church to see an example of a restoration project that should not have been funded. The building is locked, but a caretaker with the key is usually nearby. During my visit, the caretaker's young son unlocked the door for me. The church interior had white plaster walls, and featured an empty display case, suggesting that the funders of the project may have intended the church to be used as a museum.

To get there, travel west from Edremit on the main road near the shore of Lake Van. West of the Merit Sahmaran Hotel on the lake shore road, there is a big cement factory. Turn left (south, away from the lake) at this factory. This turnoff will lead up a hill to the "renovated" Armenian Church. The missing cemetery is nearby, as well.

LAKE VAN

Lake Van is one of the three great lakes of the **Armenian Plateau**. The others are Lake Sevan in Armenia and Lake Urmia in Iran. By fate of history, each of these lakes is today in a different republic.

Lake Van is in the geographic center of the Armenian Plateau, a region that also been known throughout the ages by the geographic term **Armenian Highland**. Van is the largest lake in today's Republic of Turkey, and covers an area of almost 1,500 square miles. The lake lies about 5,600 feet above sea level, and is 75 miles long and 40 miles wide at its two broadest points.

The lake is deep—at its deepest it measures 451 meters—and it's also salty. Lake Van has so much sodium carbonate and other salts that only one species of fish, the Pearl Mullet, is able to survive in its waters. This salt has two incidental effects: recreational swimmers are able to float effortlessly, and, the water is an effective detergent.

Lake Sevan, also on the Armenian Plateau, is in today's Republic of Armenia and is the easternmost of the three great lakes. Sevan, unlike Lake Van, is a fresh water lake—and is one of the largest fresh water alpine lakes in the world.

Lake Urmia, in the southeastern region of the Armenian Plateau, completes the triangle of the three great lakes of the Armenian Highland. This lake is located in today's Republic of Iran.

THE ISLANDS OF LAKE VAN

There are four islands on Lake Van. Given the penchant of Armenians for building monasteries in remote and defensible locations, it is perhaps not surprising that there is an Armenian monastery on each of them.

Aghtamar Island is the closest of the four to Van and is easily accessible by ferry from the boat launch at the town of Gevash. This is the only island that can be reached with public transportation and so it is also, understandably, the most visited of the four islands.

Lake Van

Almost no one goes to **Arter Island**, which is located just west of Aghtamar. This island might get more visitors if it had a proper dock. Instead, privately chartered boats must drop anchor near its rocky shore. Arter Island is today known in Turkey by its Turkish name, Kuşadası Island.

Lim Island is the most distant from Van, and is located in the far northeast section of the lake. There's no public boat service to Lim, but the island has a large dock that can accommodate most private boats.

Ktuts Island is close to shore and is sited near the center of the lake's eastern shoreline, just north of the town of Van. The island almost appears to be close enough to reach by swimming, but it's not. There are no public boats that make the journey to the island, but there is a large modern dock as well as a beach that is easy to moor off.

The monasteries on the islands of Arter, Lim, and Ktuts are challenging to visit because there is no public transportation available. Still, they are not off limits, and if you charter a private boat you might be able to visit them all in one long day. Private boat excursions might be possible to arrange with the boat masters at the Gevash launch, or through the concierge at one of the larger hotels. With a group of traveling companions the cost of chartering a private boat for the day can be affordable.

AGHTAMAR

The most famous of the monasteries on the islands of Lake Van, and the one that is in the best condition today, is **Aghtamar**. This monastery is located on the island of the same name near the southeast shore of the lake.

The **Cathedral of the Holy Cross**, which is known to Armenians as **Soorp Khatch**, is the gemstone of Aghtamar. This building was the cathedral of the monastery, and it is the only building of the monastic complex to have survived intact through the ages. Today, most people use the name Aghtamar as shorthand to refer to everything here—the island, the monastery, and the cathedral.

Soorp Khatch is architecturally unique among Armenian cathedrals because of the stone carvings on the exterior of the building. The carvings depict scenes from the Old and the New Testaments of the Bible, as well as secular scenes. No other Armenian church in the world is adorned as exquisitely and as extensively as Aghtamar.

This is also one of the most sacred sites of the Armenian Church. The Cathedral was built in the tenth century during the reign of **King Gagik of Vaspurakan** and has at times been the seat of the Catholicosate of the Armenian Church.

There have been additions and modifications to the buildings of Aghtamar over the centuries. A bell tower was added a couple of centuries ago. In 1951, a Turkish plan to raze the Cathedral was averted when a prominent and influential Kurdish writer intervened to save the structure.

More recently, a so-called "restoration" was completed. Both the addition of the bell tower, and the current renovations, have been justly criticized. Notwithstanding these and other so-called improvements to the structure, the Cathedral of Soorp Khatch at Aghtamar has remained structurally sound for its thousand-year history.

The rest of the monastic complex at Aghtamar hasn't fared as well. One thousand years ago, the Island of Aghtamar was an extensively developed area with orchards, gardens, and numerous monastic buildings. The Cathedral of Soorp Khatch is the oldest building that has survived to this day. There is also a ruined fourteenth century chapel located just east of the Cathedral.

Aghtamar is a popular religious pilgrimage site for Christians of all nations, as well as for Armenians. It would be unheard of for an Armenian to travel to Van without also visiting Aghtamar.

The island is also a popular secular picnic ground for many of the Kurdish people from the region. To avoid these sometimes-boisterous picnickers, and to have the island (almost) to yourself, visit Aghtamar on a weekday morning. Regardless of when you go, plan to spend at least one half day on the island viewing the cathedral, the surrounding ruins, and the many *khatchkars* in the church yard.

Soorp Khatch
(The Church of the Holy Cross)
at Aghtamar Island

World Heritage Status for Aghtamar

The entire site of Aghtamar could one day become a candidate for inclusion on the United Nations list of World Heritage sites. In 2014 the Culture and Tourism Directorate of Van asked the General Museum Directorate of Turkey to nominate Aghtamar for inclusion as a World Heritage Site.

If Aghtamar is added to this list, it could become the first exclusively Armenian site in today's Turkey with this distinction.

The historic city of Ani has been on a "tentative" list of World Heritage sites since 2012, but Turkey's nomination of Ani treats Ani as a multicultural, and not an Armenian, site, despite the wealth of historic evidence that shows Ani to have been Armenian.

In 1972, the United Nations Educational, Scientific and Cultural Organization (UNESCO) adopted a treaty known as the World Heritage Convention. The organization recruits the world community in identifying cultural and natural properties of "outstanding universal value." A site must be nominated by the host government to be considered for inclusion on the World Heritage list.

Certainly Aghtamar seems to fit the bill for inclusion on the list. There are 13 World Heritage sites in today's Turkey, and three in the Republic of Armenia. The Armenia sites are (1) the Cathedral and Churches of Echmiadzin and the Archaeological Site of Zvartnots; (2) the Monastery of Geghardt and the Upper Azat Valley; and (3) the Monasteries of Haghpat and Sanahin.

Aghtamar, 1997

Aghtamar reliefs

The Plan to Demolish Aghtamar

During an apparent frenzy of destruction during the 1950s, numerous Armenian churches were destroyed throughout Turkey. Aghtamar was almost one of them.

In 1951, a plan to demolish Aghtamar had been put into effect. A small chapel next to the Cathedral had already been destroyed when the scheme came to the attention of Yasar Kemal, a prominent and influential Kurdish writer from the region.

Yasar Kemal complained to a military officer about the impending destruction, and implored him to save Aghtamar. He appealed to the officer's sense of patriotism by describing Aghtamar as a monument of Anatolia.

The writer and the military officer traveled to Aghtamar the following day, and they both observed that the destruction was indeed imminent. The military officer became angered and he ordered the workers to stop. The order to save Aghtamar took effect on June 25, 1951.

The 'Restoration' of Aghtamar

The **Cathedral of Soorp Khatch** on the Island of **Aghtamar** is one of Armenia's most beautiful churches. The building is architecturally unique among Armenian churches because of the elaborate and extensive carvings that adorn all four sides of its façade. The site is also historically significant as a past seat of the Catholicosate of the Armenian Church.

Aghtamar reliefs

Aghtamar frescoes

Altar at Aghtamar

Accordingly, Aghtamar is probably the best known, the most-visited, and the most highly revered among all the Armenian churches of historic Armenia.

Soorp Khatch was built during the years 915 to 921, during the reign of King Gagik of Vaspurakan and this is certainly King Gagik's most famous architectural legacy.

This architectural legacy has not gone unaltered over the years, however. A church hall, known as a *gavit*, was added to the building in 1763. A bell tower was added to the east portico of the building in the nineteenth century. An original tenth century staircase on the exterior of the building was removed in order to make room for the bell tower. This addition also damaged some of the stone carvings on the exterior wall of Soorp Khatch.

More recently, the Turkish government has been restoring the site. This "restoration" began in 2006 and is connected with the decision of the Turkish authorities to declare that Aghtamar is a state-owned museum. A sign was posted on the island in 2014 that announced, fot the first time, that Aghtamar is Armenian.

Critics of the restoration at Aghtamar contend that the work is not faithful to the original architectural design of the building. They say that the restoration has caused damage, and that the entire project is politically motivated.

The architecture experts who operate the Virtual Ani project, for example, report that removing the grass roof from the building's meeting hall and replacing it with concrete and stone will cause long-term damage to the building from trapped moisture. They also point to the replacement of worn floor tiles with machine-hewn stones as a restoration that is not faithful to the original design.

Many Armenians also believe that the decision of the Turkish government to restore Aghtamar was unnecessary, and that it is politically inspired. These critics contend that the construction work is window dressing that has been undertaken so that the Turkish government can appear to be a benevolent authority.

Van

The restoration is therefore said to be an attempt to appease critics who have accused Turkey of destroying, either intentionally or through neglect, hundreds of ancient Armenian churches throughout the country.

The value of the restoration and the motivation for the construction work can probably be debated. The re-purposing of Aghtamar by the Turkish government as a secular Turkish museum is beyond debate, however, and cannot be justified or rationalized. Aghtamar is a sacred Armenian church of infinite cultural value to the Armenian nation.

Aghtamar was seized from the Armenian Church after 1915, because it was supposedly "abandoned" by the victims of the genocide. The island and its priceless monastic complex should be returned to the Armenian Church as the first small step toward Turkey's atonement for the genocide.

For the best photography, visit late in the day when you can photograph the sun shining on Soorp Khatch with the mountain, Mount Artos, in the background. Plan to make your photographs shortly *before* sunset. A large hill on the island west of the Cathedral will block the setting sun during the final hour of the day. Be aware that photographers are sometimes told that they are not allowed to use tripods on the island.

Aghtamar Island is the easiest to visit of the four islands on Lake Van. There's a public boat launch from the town of Gevash, which is about 35 kilometers west of Van. Throughout the day several boats are on-hand to make the simple 20-minute journey from Gevash to Aghtamar.

To get there (Aghtamar) from Van take a *dolmus*, (public minivan), to the Gevash boat launch. The *dolmus* fare varies by distance, and from Van should be less than $3. Avoid using a taxi, which can cost $90 each way. After visiting Aghtamar, if you plan to return to Van by dolmus, then plan to be on the road before sunset. There are fewer mini-vans available at night, and many (but not all of them) don't operate later than 6 pm.

From Gevash, the boat operators typically charge a minimum of $50 for each boat trip to Aghtamar. So if there are ten (or more) passengers on your boat, your individual fare will be just $5. The boat will depart when it is full, or when the boat captain is satisfied with the number of tickets he has sold. Departures to the island usually begin at around 9 am. Returns are throughout the day until sunset. No ticket or additional payment is required for the return trip.

Aghtamar is a sacred Armenian religious site, but the authorities who have custody today operate it as a state-run museum. You will therefore be required to pay an entrance fee (about $2.50) when you arrive on the island. Praying aloud and singing hymns in the church is also forbidden, but visitors can usually find creative ways to overcome this restriction.

Khatchkar at Aghtamar

Armenian clerics during the
annual Liturgy at Aghtamar

THE DIVINE LITURGY AT AGHTAMAR

The Divine Liturgy of the Armenian Church has been officially performed *once* each year at Aghtamar since 2010. Prior to 2010, this church service, which the Armenians refer to as the *badarak*, had not been openly performed at Aghtamar *at all* since 1915.

Three years later, in September 2013, and also for the first time in nearly a century, the Armenian Church performed the rite of baptism here, immediately following the annual *badarak*. More than one thousand pilgrims attended the religious ceremony on that day. I was one of them.

The observation of church services and baptisms at Aghtamar is an unusual event.

This is because the Turkish government, which seized this majestic cathedral from the Armenians in 1915, had not allowed Armenians to pray or to worship there for most of the past century.

Armenians do sometimes pray and worship and sing in the church. I know this. I was at Aghtamar in 1997 when Mesrob Ashjian, an archbishop of the Armenian Church, sang the *Hayr Mer* (Lord's Prayer). I'm sure others have done this, too. But these prayers have always been done secretly, and furtively, and never with official tolerance of the government, which considers itself to be the owner of Aghtamar.

So the first publicly sanctioned *badarak* in 2010 was a big deal. And when the first baptisms in almost a century were held at Aghtamar in 2013, I decided to go.

I discovered that I was not the only person who had traveled from afar to attend the baptisms. I met a group of Armenians who had made the journey from Australia. One of these Australian Armenians explained that attending the *badarak* at Aghtamar was a dream for her and her family. "We have all been to Armenia," she told me, "but not this part of Armenia."

The Armenians who made the shortest pilgrimage to Aghtamar on that day were from the town of Van. These Armenians were amongst the hidden Armenians of the region—Armenians who still live in the area but who conceal their identity in order to survive without persecution. One of them was baptized at Aghtamar on that day.

I spent about twelve hours on Aghtamar Island, from sunrise, until sunset, from before the *badarak*, until long after the baptized Armenians, hidden and not hidden, had gone home. The sun had finally stopped shining on Aghtamar and the last boat back to shore was ready to depart, so I walked back to the harbor.

As my boat chugged along back to Van, it occurred to me that the expression of Armenian culture at Aghtamar was starting another yearlong hibernation. But I was happy that for one long day, the sun had shined bright, the island had been alive, and that Soorp Khatch had been, once again, an Armenian cathedral.

The first baptisms at Aghtamar in 100 years

The island of Aghtamar

RETURN THE ARMENIAN CHURCHES

Thousands of churches in Western Armenia are today "owned" by Turkey's government, by Turkey's military, and even in some cases by private individuals.

The Church of the Holy Cross (Soorp Khatch) at Aghtamar is perhaps the most prominent of the Armenian churches that Turkey today claims to own.

The legal basis for the Turkish ownership claims is typically the same. The original Armenian owners supposedly abandoned the properties in 1915 or shortly thereafter. Once the properties were abandoned, the state was free to step in and confiscate them.

Turkey's seizures were pursuant to the letter of their law. In 1923, the newly established Republic of Turkey enacted a law that allowed the government to seize the property of any Armenian who was not present on his property. The law did not make any allowance for the reason the owner was absent.

Thus, Aghtamar, which was built by the Armenians in 915 and which was operated as an Armenian cathedral for the next thousand years, was seized as an abandoned property shortly after the genocide of 1915.

Turkey had planned to demolish Aghtamar back in 1951. By 2007 it had decided to instead renovate the site and repurpose the cathedral as a state-operated secular museum. This was supposed to be a public relations boost to Turkey. But instead, it's been a disaster. Turkey's decision to turn Aghtamar into a museum had the unintended effect of shining a bright light on the issue of all church seizures.

A legal and political campaign to compel Turkey to return Aghtamar and other Armenian churches to the Armenians was commenced. Even the two leaders of the politically fractured Armenian Church put aside their differences in 2013 and jointly called upon Turkey to return all seized churches.

By 2015, only Soorp Giragos in Diyarbakir had been returned to the Armenian people. But Aghtamar has remained a focal point for a growing movement to compel Turkey to return Armenia's stolen churches to the Armenians.

Soorp Khatch as it appeared in 1997

ARTER ISLAND

Arter Island, home to the eponymous **Arterivank**, is located just four kilometers west of Aghtamar Island. The island receives few visitors despite its proximity to the super-popular Aghtamar, however. This is mostly because there's no public transportation to Arter. Private boat operators also report that it is frequently difficult to moor at the island because of strong winds and water currents. The island is uninhabited and has neither a harbor nor a dock.

The origin of the monastery is unclear. One account links **Gregory of Narek** to its establishment. According to this story, Gregory had a vision during the tenth century that he interpreted as the image of the Virgin Mary and Baby Jesus sitting in the clouds above the island.

He responded by running from the monastery of Narekavank, and across the waters of Lake Van, until he reached the island. It isn't clear if he also ran across the water to get back. In any event, the monastery of Arterivank was founded some time later, perhaps as much as two centuries later, to commemorate Narek's vision.

There was once an inscription on the island bearing the date 1292, and which therefore constituted at least some evidence that the monastery may have existed here in the thirteenth century. The stone bearing this inscription is now missing.

Today all that survives of the monastic complex is one church, which is known as the **Mother of God**. A second church that was

Lake Van

known to exist at the monastery no longer exists. West of the church there are today some ruins, mostly foundation stones, from other buildings that had once been part of the monastery. The surviving church sits on the ridge of the island, making it clearly visible from a great distance.

Arterivank was restored during the late eighteenth century but was closed shortly after this restoration when the leader of the monastery, a Vardabed named James, was arrested and tortured.

LIM ISLAND

Lim Island is the farthest from Van of the four islands on Lake Van. The island is known today by its Turkish name, Adir Adasi, or Adir Island.

This island was the site, in the fourteenth century, of the Hermitage of **Soorp Gevorg (St. George)**. The monastery was built as early as 1305 and was expanded to accommodate the growing needs of the local Armenian community in the seventeenth and eighteenth centuries. The site once boasted its main church, Soorp Gevorg, as well as a meeting hall, bell tower, monk's cells, and a guesthouse, as well as a large cemetery.

When I traveled to the island, I saw the ruins of the monastic complex, which had been reduced to a structure that looked like a square jewel box. The surviving church had a partly intact roof, but it had no dome or drum.

Thousands of Armenians used this island as a refuge in 1915. When Turkish forces learned that Armenians were hiding on the

The monastery on Lim Island

island, they took measures to ensure that they could not leave. By some accounts, roughly 12,000 women and children starved to death while stranded on Lim Island.

Today the island is uninhabited, arid, and stark. The status of the island as an island of death in 1915 made it unpleasantly appropriate during my visit that I needed to step over the carcasses of hundreds of dead gulls that had apparently chosen Lim Island as their final resting place.

A large public dock in good repair easily accommodated our privately chartered boat, but traveling here required a big investment of time and money. Travel time from Van, using a fast boat, was about four hours. Because of the difficulty of access, and because the site is so badly ruined, this island will be of interest primarily to the serious student of Armenian history.

KTUTS ISLAND

Ktuts Island is home to a beautifully sited fifteenth century monastery. The island is so named because its peninsula—a prominent feature of the island's topography—is shaped like the beak of a bird. Ktuts is the Armenian word for a bird's beak.

Ruins from the monastery, including the remnants of monks' cells and a cemetery, are still present. The main church that is standing on the island today, **Soorp Garabed**, was built in the early eighteenth century.

This church is in remarkably good repair considering that it has endured one hundred years of vandalism and neglect, and has not had any maintenance since 1915.

The complex here originally featured, in addition to the church, a meeting hall, a bell tower, a cemetery, and a large residential building. The residences and the cemetery disappeared during the past century, but the church, the hall, and part of the bell tower are still present.

Ktuts Island

In a departure from the preferences typically selected for the siting of churches, this church is not perched on a defensible hilltop, but rather is beautifully sited near the shore of Lake Van at the base of a hill. The presence of the monastery on a remote island may have helped to reduce the amount of damage that it has suffered since 1915.

Ktuts Island is parched and dry in late summer and in the autumn. By August, the vegetation is brown and lifeless. This is in great contrast to the scenery in the spring, when the island is teeming with the saturated reds and yellows of poppies and wild flowers, and when tall green grasses sway in the breeze.

Travelers in late spring will encounter nesting gulls, which commandeer the island for several weeks while they lay eggs and tend to their offspring. If you travel to Ktuts during nesting season, be careful not to walk on the hundreds of nests that the birds have built on the ground, and use caution to avoid being attacked by the gulls, which will swoop down upon intruders and defecate on them to keep them away from their nesting eggs. During my visit I found it helpful to keep my head down.

For the best photography, arrive in early morning. A large hill west of the church will obstruct the late-day sun. Climb to the top of this hill for images that show both the church, and also the "beak" of the island. This is where I stood in order to create the photograph on the cover of this book.

To get there, you need to hire a private boat. There is no public transportation. Ktuts is located northwest of the town of Van, roughly at the center of the eastern shore of Lake Van. To find a boat, check with the boat masters at Gevash, or with the concierge at your hotel. Allow several hours for this visit. Because you will need to hire a boat, this island is not easy to reach. But the visit is worthwhile and is recommended.

The **Monastery of Soorp Gevorg (St. George) of Goms** is not located on any of the four islands of Lake Van. Still, the site is probably most easily reached by boat. This is because the monastery is on a remote part of the Lake Van shoreline, in the district of Gevash, and is otherwise accessible only by a steep trail. During my visit to the site, I arrived on a privately chartered boat, which added to the drama of the visit.

The monastery is believed to have been built by King Gagik of Vaspurakan, probably in AD 905. Goms is the nearest village to the monastery, which is sometimes called **Gomkavank**. This village exists today by the Kurdish name Kumus. Turkish maps show the town's name as Canakduzu.

There's little historical information available for this site, but one source suggests that the head of the saint after whom this monastery was named may have been kept here.

The church of the monastery, which is also named Soorp Gevorg, is accessed by one door on the west side of the structure and is surrounded by a stone wall which was repaired in 1760, according to an inscription. None of the other buildings of the monastery has survived. Photographs from 1972 make it evident that this thousand year old church has been heavily damaged during the past forty years.

Soorp Gevorg was abandoned in 1830 because it had become difficult to defend from Kurdish raids. The isolated location of the monastery had, for a time, helped it to avoid destruction during the decades after 1915. Now, the rising level of Lake Van threatens to erode the foundation of the structure. The church is on a short bluff, just several feet from the water.

To get there, you have two difficult options for this hard-to-reach site. If you charter a private boat, you can reach this shoreline church by sailing west from Aghtamar, for roughly three hours. If you travel overland, which is preferable, you'll need to first travel to the valley of Goms, which is known in Turkish as Gollu Ovasi ("the plain with the lake"), and find the trail that leads down to the monastery. Either route will be an adventure that is best left to the heartiest of adventurers. **GPS map coordinates** for Soorp Gevorg of Goms: 38° 28' 54.59" N 42° 37' 54.64" E

Kfuls Island

THE REGION OF VAN

Most of the churches and monasteries in the region of Van that have survived since 1915 are in remote locations. Some are on isolated hilltops that can be reached only after long hikes that require both strength and stamina. Others are secluded in villages and have been forgotten or adapted to other uses.

The difficulty of getting to some sites might account for their survival to this day. Ultimately, however, during the century following 1915, fortuity may be the only explanation for why one church was destroyed and another was spared.

Karmravank and **Soorp Tovmas** are ancient monasteries located on neighboring hilltops. They each deserve to be visited. The ruins of these monasteries are each located about a ninety-minute drive from the town of Van, in the district of Gevash, which is west of Van. You can visit both of these sites in a single day-trip from Van.

According to legend, Karmravank was until 1895 a repository of part of the cross upon which Jesus had been crucified. Karmravank and its treasures were plundered by a Kurdish tribe in 1895, during an exceptionally troubled year when Turkish authorities had sanctioned massacres of Armenians throughout the Ottoman Empire.

The fragment of the cross was lost during the plunder. Another relic of the so-called "true cross" upon which Jesus was crucified would be lost from another Armenian church, twenty years later in 1915, during the siege of Van by the Turkish Army.

The name Karmravank alludes to the reddish color of the brick drum of the monastery's Church of Soorp Nishan. *Karmir* is the Armenian word for red. The literal translation of Karmravank is red monastery. In Turkey today the site is known as Gorundu Kilisesi or Gorundu Church. Gorundu is the name of the nearby village.

The use of brick as a construction material for the drum of this church is unusual. Most Armenian churches, and their drums, are constructed from stone. The drum, which is the circular part of the roof that supports the conical dome, is noteworthy for another

reason, as well: there's a gaping hole in one side, which was apparently created by a cannon ball or by some other explosive.

This is another of the monasteries that is believed to have been founded by King Gagik of Vaspurakan in the tenth century, although some sources date the monastery to the twelfth century. The church that survives at this location today, however, probably dates to the fifteenth century. King Gagik is also credited with founding the monastery on Aghtamar Island.

When I visited this church, I observed that the floor of the church near the entry and near the altar had been crudely excavated. This excavation had exposed part of the foundation. These holes are a common sight at abandoned Armenian churches. Treasure hunters believe that gold is buried beneath the entryways and beneath the altars of Armenian churches.

There's no treasure, of course, and when these bandits make this disappointing discovery, they depart without restoring the ground that they disturbed. The result is that this church, and others, have exposed foundations that place the buildings at risk of collapse.

Soorp Tovmas, which is also known as **St. Thomas**, is located on a hilltop just past Karmravank. This once majestic monastery dates back to the tenth or eleventh centuries, and is perched near the top of a barren hill overlooking Lake Van. The monastery is located near the old Armenian town of Gandzak, which is today known by its new Turkish name, Altinsac.

The complex has undergone two restorations. The drum of the church was rebuilt in 1581, and the entire exterior was restored in 1801. The architect Nairy Hampikian describes Soorp Tovmas as having a decorative manner that is associated with Persian aesthetics.

There is a plundered cemetery with ancient *khatchkars* located just behind the church, a bit farther up the hill. Some of the graves appeared to have been freshly disturbed when I photographed them in recent years.

Soorp Tovmas

Karmravank and Soorp Tovmas are located on separate hilltops, and hiking to either of them requires stamina and endurance. If you are hiking in the summer, start with plenty of water, and with protection from the strong sun. The hike to Karmravank follows a dirt trail and is not exceptionally difficult.

Hiking to Soorp Tovmas will take close to one hour. If you have time to visit only one of these sites, choose Soorp Tovmas, because of its dramatic setting with stunning views of Lake Van, and because of the nearby cemetery of *khatchkars*.

For the best photography, visit Soorp Tovmas in mid-to-late afternoon, when the sun will be setting behind the church and illuminating Lake Van to the east. You can take advantage of the location of the sun to place Lake Van in the background of your images. If you visit in the morning, the sun will be above the lake.

To get there, travel west from Van for about 45 minutes along the main highway that follows the Lake Van shoreline. Turn right (north) at the signposted turnoff for the village of Altinsac. Altinsac is the new Turkish name for the ancient Armenian village of Ganjak. This road is paved, and in parts it is not quite wide enough for two cars to pass. Stay on this narrow road for about 45 minutes as it winds along the shore of Lake Van, through the village of Altinsac.

Karmravank is located on a hilltop west of this road, and Soorp Tovmas is located on a second hilltop, just past Karmravank, and also on the west side of the road. The hike to Karmravank is strenuous but can be completed in about 30 minutes by a person in reasonably good shape. The hike to Soorp Tovmas is longer and steeper, and takes about 60 minutes. Neither trek requires any

Karmravank

special hiking skills or equipment, apart from water, sunblock, and stamina. **GPS map coordinates** for Soorp Tovmas: 38° 25'0.42" N 42° 52'26.80" E. **GPS map coordinates** for Karmravank: 38° 22'20.42" N 42° 54'14.88" E

In the village of **Altinsac** there is the ruin of a small Armenian church, with *khatchkars*, that dates from the fifteenth or sixteenth century. This church is worth a short stop on the way to either Karmravank or Soorp Tovmas.

Just west of Altinsac, and also on the Lake Van shoreline, the church of **Soorp Hovhannes** has escaped destruction and is still standing with its roof and walls intact. This is a good achievement, considering that this building has not been properly maintained since it was abandoned a century ago.

The church is the only surviving structure of the monastic complex of **Soorp Garabed**, which some sources identify by the name **Sorbayvank**. Soorp Garabed is dramatically sited on a bluff overlooking Lake Van. The local villagers are using this church for storage.

To get there, travel to the village that is today known by the Turkish name Yelkenli. This is the former Armenian village of Soorp. **GPS map coordinates** for Soorp Hovhannes Church: 38° 29' 38.99" N 42° 32'48.92" E

The Monastery of **Soorp Marinos** is easy to locate, but difficult to reach because of its location atop a steep hilltop, accessible only by foot on a dirt trail. This site is southwest of the town of Van, near the village of Arkboyu, in the region of historic Armenia that is

A Kurdish villager at Soorp Hovhannes

Soorp Marinos

known as **Hayots Dzor**, or the **Valley of the Armenians**. This valley earned its name at the beginning of Armenian history, when Hayk, the legendary father of the Armenian nation, arrived in this area.

Although the exact date of the founding of this monastery is unknown, the structures that survive here may date back to the ninth century. Monks here are known to have created manuscripts during the sixteenth century. Some of these manuscripts have survived and are now in custody of the Matenadaran—Armenia's repository of manuscripts—in Yerevan.

Soorp Marinos is in ruins today, but it must have once been a grand site. As recently as the nineteenth century, the monastery was the occasional home to the Catholicos—the leader of the Armenian Church. Childless women made pilgrimage to this site, presumably to assist them with their fertility.

To get there, drive west from Van, and take the south turnoff that is signposted for Bashkale. After taking this turnoff, drive south for 13.5 kilometers, in the direction of Bashkale. At the 13.5-kilometer mark, take the left turnoff toward the mountain. This road takes you past a small village, where the road becomes rough and unpaved.

Drive toward the mountain as far as this road will take you, just past the village of Arkboyu. Travel time by car is about 45 minutes. Hike the rest of the way, which will take about 60 minutes. This trek does not require special skills or equipment, but it does require endurance. Do not attempt this hike unless you are in good physical condition. **GPS map coordinates** for Soorp Marinos: 38° 20' 44.46" N 43° 21' 23.81" E

Soorp Bartholomew is located south of the town of Van, in the town of Albayrak, and exudes great historic significance. Soorp

Soorp Bartholomew

Bartholomew, together with Soorp Thaddeus, are the two apostles who are credited with bringing Christianity to Armenia, and who are thus revered as pillars of the Armenian Apostolic Church.

St. Thaddeus was also honored with a church and monastery which is located nearby, but across the frontier in the territory of today's Islamic Republic of Iran. Visiting the monasteries of both Soorp Bartholomew and Soorp Thaddeus in one day-trip is therefore not possible.

The monastery of Soorp Bartholomew is built upon a hill site where St. Bartholomew is believed to have perished. Albayrak, which takes its name from the Turkish word for flag, was previously known as Deir, which is the Kurdish word for monastery.

You can visit Soorp Bartholomew, and also the nearby **Soorp Echmiadzin** (described on p. 123), in a single day-trip from the town of Van. There is no hiking required for either site.

Soorp Bartholomew is sited near the Turkey-Iran border and was until recently inaccessible because of its location in a restricted military zone, entirely within a Turkish military base.

The base was relocated outside of town in 2012 and access to the church was restored in July 2013. I visited Soorp Bartholomew in September 2013, just a few weeks after the restrictions on visiting had been lifted. A barbed wire gate was still in place, but has since been removed.

The monastery dates back to the sixth century, and was in active use until 1915. A large hall was added at the front entrance in the thirteenth century, and this hall is still standing, although without its roof.

The architecture historian Nairy Hampikian describes the architecture that supported the roof at Soorp Bartholomew. "Two columns and six pillars [are] set against the internal walls of the hall [and] carry four crossing arches which create the base for the covering of the hall." This design is a variation of the small side niches of Soorp Khatch at Aghtamar, according to Hampikian.

Soorp Bartholomew entryway

Soorp Echmiadzin

The roof, as well as its drums and conical domes, are all missing. They had been intact until 1915, and photographs show that the fifteen hundred year-old monastery had an intact roof at least until 1911. Visitors have reported seeing the roof intact, with its dome, in the early 1960s. An earthquake in 1966 caused extensive damage to the surviving church, however, and this may have been when the domes were lost.

About 60 kilometers from Van, near the town of Guzelsu on the road toward Soorp Bartholomew, you will pass the famous **Hoshap Castle**. Most of the castle standing today dates back to 1643 and was built by a local Kurdish ruler. Armenians are believed to have built some original parts of the castle during the medieval period.

To get there, travel south from the town of Van, past the Hoshap castle, and in the direction of Bashkale. Take the left turnoff toward the village of Albaryak. Soorp Bartholomew is located just off the main roadway, near the center of the village, about 100 kilometers from Van. Travel time from Van is about 90 minutes. **GPS map coordinates** for Soorp Bartholomew: 38 8' 58" N, 44 12' 48" E

Soorp Echmiadzin is located about 22 kilometers past Soorp Bartholomew, in the town of Aghbak, a town that is today known by the Turkish name Yanal. The village was once known as Soradir or Zoradir and the church is also known as Soorp Khatch (the Church of the Holy Cross). This sixth century church was built by an apprentice of the architect who constructed Soorp Bartholomew, a short time later.

Inscriptions found inside this church attest to its construction in AD 582. The church is architecturally significant for its design, which served as a model for Aghtamar, which was built roughly three hundred years later.

The architecture historian Nairy Hampikian writes that this repetition of design illustrates the existence of a "cultural memory" of Armenian church architecture through the ages.

A Kurdish village has grown up around Soorp Echmiadzin, but there is still a large grassy yard surrounding the building. At the rear of this yard there is a row of *khatchkars*, some of which have been used in a retaining wall.

To get there, after reaching Soorp Bartholomew, travel 22 kilometers farther on the main road. There are a couple of forks in the road that can cause confusion, so ask for directions to the town of Yanal, which is the current name of the village in which Soorp Echmiadzin is located. **GPS map coordinates** for Soorp Echmiadzin: 38° 15' 46.31"N 44° 15' 8.66"E

Region of Moks

The region of **Moks** is home to the ruins of several Armenian churches. Moks is a large and remote area, located south of Lake Van, about 100 kilometers southwest of the town of Van. The current Turkish name for the area is Bahcesaray.

Seventy-five percent of the population here was Armenian just prior to 1915. The rest were Kurds. Today the region's populace is entirely Kurdish.

Exploring the abandoned Armenian sites of the Moks region can be challenging. Most of the churches are sequestered on mountaintops and hilltops and often can be reached only by hiking. The communities within this large region each tended to have their own church, so there's a lot to see (or look for). Another result of this individualism, however, is an abundance of structures without great architectural distinction. All of this makes Moks a destination that is compelling and brimming with history, but still not a first-choice for many pilgrims.

The **Monastery of Soorp Khatch (Holy Cross)** is a highlight of the region. Soorp Khatch is located near the village of **Aparank**, and may have been founded as early as the tenth century. The surviving church dates back to the fifteenth century.

The most famous religious relic of the monastery was an arm (yes, an arm) of St. John the Baptist. The arm had apparently been kept in a bronze case that was shaped to resemble the arm. Today this relic is no longer here, and may be at a church in Iran.

Lake Van as viewed from Soorp Tovmas

Soorp Bartholomew as seen from the rear

GETTING TO VAN

There are several flights to Van each day from Istanbul and Ankara. All domestic flights in Turkey use Istanbul or Ankara as a hub so it is not possible to fly directly into or out of Van from any city other than Istanbul or Ankara. The Van airport is about 5 kilometers outside the city and is served by mini vans as well as taxis.

Van's bus station, the *otogar*, is just outside the city limits, about four kilometers past the center of town along the east (right) side of the roadway that leads toward Dogubeyazit. Buses provide service from this bus station to most major cities of historic Armenia, including to Diyarbakir, Tatvan, Erzerum, Dogubeyazit, and Kars.

When to Visit

Visitors in September can attend the annual *badarak* at Aghtamar, which since 2010 has been held during the first two weeks of the month. September also offers the most temperate climate. For the best weather, go between late May and late September.

Suggested Itinerary

This suggested itinerary covers the highlights of the Van region, in roughly the order of significance of the sites, so that you can plan a visit of from one to five days.

1. Day One: Sunrise at the ruins of Old Van and climbing the Rock of Van; afternoon at Aghtamar until late afternoon or until just before sunset.

2. Day Two: Morning at Church of Soorp Hovhannes (Soorp Garabed Monastery) on the Lake Van shoreline, located just west of Altinsac; then in afternoon the strenuous hikes to Soorp Tovmas and Karmravank.

3. Day Three: Hoshap Castle, S. Bartholomew, and S. Echmiadzin.

4. Day Four: Private boat to the island of Ktuts in early morning; afternoon at Varagavank and Edremit.

5. Day Five: Region of Moks.

Karmravank

Diyarbakir, Bitlis and Erzerum

The Monastery of Nine Tombs in the region of Erzerum

PLAIN of MUSH (DARŌN)

L. Nazik

PERTEK
VAZGERT
Peri
CHAPAKJUR
Murat (Aratzani or Eastern Euphrates)
GENCH
Huyot
KULP
Sekilda
3047 /
Nemrut
3117 / 9500
L. Nemrut

KEBAN
MADEN

HARPUT
(KHARPERT)
Mezraa
(Mëzirë)

MUSH

Palu
Kaghts'raheayats' V.
(Havav)
PALU
(Akrag)

(Havri)
Sarikamish
(Vartenik')
Nacharan
(Nakran)

Kurdemini
Günei (Guney)
S. Nshan Tzovamoyn
(Island mon.)
(Hayrat'of)
Haftasar (Hawtasar)
L. Güljik [Tzovk']
Göljük (Tsovk' kiugh)
(Gaysrig)
(Partsunk')
Zibene
(Tigris)
Topalan
(T'opelan)
Dibni (Debne)
Berbas
(Barbesh)
Birkleyn [Anc. Illyrison]
LIJE
Cheper han [Anc. Saphkhai]
SASUN
MOTKAN /
MUTKI

BITLIS
(PAGHESH)

SANJAK of ERGANI
Norshin
(Norashën)
Telbaghdad
(T'il-Baghdad)
ARZNI / ARGHANA
ARNI
Hayni
Lije
Zara
Hezan (Hazan)
Kervas (Garvas/Garas)
Magapayets'voc' V. / Magavank'
Sasun

HAZO / HAZRO
Hazo

Sirahayeats'
S. Asdvatzatzin
(Adish)
Salvaz (Spidag)
2055 / 6677
Piran
ERGANI
Payanle (Payan)
Eghil (Ankgh)
S. Nshan
Terevenk
(Tëravank')
Intak / Aintak (Ant'ag / Ant'agh / At'akh) [Anc. Attakhas]
Dakyanus Kal'e /
(Kilise) 2055 / 4757
(Fis) [Anc. Pheison]

Chüngüsh
(Chunkush)
Partsrahayeats'
Asdvatzatzin V.
CHERMIK (CHERMUG)
Malan (Milan)
(T'arji)
(Parpush)
Hazro

Baghvenk
(Aghmashad)
Egrek (Akrag)
Silvan
Tigris

Most likely site of ancient
Tigranakert (Dikranagerd)

KUFRE / SHIRVA

Chermik
(Khimeri)
FARKIN / SILVAN
Farkin
(Arzan)
ZOK / GARZAN
SIIRT
Ap
Bohtan

KAHTA
Gerger
Yep'rat
Sungur

Kirvan
Shemen Mts.
Siverek
Arbur
Batman

(Mama-Daud)
(Suv)
(Merton)
HASANKEYF
REDVAN
Yezidi
Kurds
DEH

Nisibin (Mësebin)
Halebi (Halëbi)
Mezre (Meghre)
Hadro
Hoshin (Khoshen /
Oshin)
SIVEREK
(SEW AVERAG /
SEVEREK)
Simag
(Simak'li / Simakhi)
Göllügölan
(Khallok'an)
Kara
Koda
Dijle
(Western Tigris)
Yezidi Kurds
Niha

DIYARBEKIR
(DIKRANAGERD)

SANJAK of DIYARBEKIR

Chatak (Chatagh)
Karbi (Khibi)
Güllü (Gori)
Karaja
1919 / 6296
Tahtkilli
1727 / 5650
Kuru
Ak
Avine
AVINE
Savur (Tzavur)
Midyat
MIDYAT
Tur Abdin (Jebel Tur)
Finik
Jerani
Tigris

Beyruk (Beyrog)
S. Taniël V.
DERIK (DIREK)
(Penapil)
JIZRE
Arab. Jezire-ibn-
Omar
Firi

Derik
MARDIN
Mar Michael
Escarpment
NUSAYBIN
(MTZPIN)
MARDIN
JIZRE

Viranshehir / Tilli
Tell Halab
Dara

SANJAK of MARDIN
Mardin
Nusaybin

RASULAYN

Scale
0   25   50 km.
0   25   50 mi.

Legend

● Vilayet (Province) Capital

◉ Sanjak (County) Capital

⊙ Kaza (District) Center

Diyarbakir Ottoman Turkish Name (Official)

(Dikranagerd) Western Armenian Name (Colloquial)

• Armenian Village

✝ Armenian Archbishop, Bishop, Prelate

✝ Armenian Catholic Archbishop, Bishop

◆ Monastery

Courtesy of Robert H. Hewsen

Diyarbakir

INTRODUCTION

Armenians revere the region of **Diyarbakir** as the home of the ancient Armenian capital of **Tigranakert**.

The exact location of Tigranakert has been lost to history, but the contributions of this city and of its founder **Tigran the Great** are a source of pride for the Armenian nation, and especially to the *Tigranakertsi*—the Armenian natives of Tigranakert.

Ancient Tigranakert was founded in 95 BC and flourished as the capital of the Armenian kingdom of Tigran the Great for just forty years, until 55 BC. Scholars are today divided on the location of Tigran's city, but the most probable location according to recent research is near the town of **Arzan**. This town is located midway between Bitlis and the modern city of Diyarbakir, and is just outside the present boundary of the province of Diyarbakir.

The modern city of Diyarbakir and its environs is, according to this same scholarly research, the *least* likely location for the old capital of Tigranakert. The ongoing scholarly debate about Tigranakert's location has not produced a conclusive finding, and there have been no archaeological excavations to support the selection of any particular site.

For the *Tigranakertsi*, the natives of Tigranakert, this uncertainty has neither mitigated their pride in, nor dampened their enthusiasm for, the glory of Diyarbakir.

During ancient times, Diyarbakir had been known as the city of **Amida**, and had been under Byzantine rule in AD 639 at the time of its capture by Arabs. Amida briefly became an Arab state, and was eventually restored to the Byzantine Empire in AD 958.

Invading Seljuks, Turkmen, and Mongols followed in waves, until the city and the surrounding region was finally conquered by the Ottoman Turks in 1516.

By 1867, when the *vilayet* (province) of Diyarbakir was established, the province had become known as one of the six Armenian provinces of the Ottoman Empire.

Most of the Armenians of this province lived either in the city of Diyarbakir or in the vast region north of the city. This sector of Diyarbakir province, laying north of the city, was within the Armenian Plateau, and was properly part of Armenia. These lands included the historic and significant Armenian areas of Palu, Chunkush, and, directly west of Diyarbakir, the town of Severek. **Palu** and **Chunkush** today have the important ruins of Armenian churches and monasteries. **Severek**, which had a population of about 5,500 Armenians just before 1915, today has no surviving Armenian monuments or ruins.

The sector of Diyarbakir province located south of the city of Diyarbakir, meanwhile, was located on the Mesopotamian plains, rather than upon the Armenian Plateau. Fewer Armenians lived in this area. This southern district was populated mostly by Kurds.

Population statistics vary, but by some accounts, by 1914, Diyarbakir had grown to a city of about 45,000 inhabitants.

The bell tower of Soorp Giragos

Its population was distributed among Turks and Kurds, Arabs and Turkmen, Armenians and Greeks. Almost one third of the population was Armenian. The rest were mostly Muslim. The Armenian Patriarchate counted some 124,000 Armenians living throughout Diyarbakir province in 1914.

Today about a million people live in Diyarbakir, including a few Armenians, some of whom are among the population of hidden Armenians. Most of the people are Kurdish, and Diyarbakir is today a cultural capital of Kurdistan in Turkey.

By all appearances, the city is Middle Eastern. The streets are narrow, and merchants and craftsmen crowd the alleys, selling herbs and spices, and crafting iron works. Pedestrians compete with chai vendors for space on the sidewalks and the attire of the locals includes veils on women and traditional baggy trousers on men.

Diyarbakir is also the center of a delicate and tepid revitalization of the Armenian community.

During the past several years there have been signs of outreach from the Kurdish community—a community that includes almost everyone in Diyarbakir—toward the descendants of the tiny minority of Armenians who somehow remained here in 1915 or who returned to Diyarbakir after the *Medz Yeghern* (Great Crime).

The Kurdish leadership of Diyarbakir has supported—both financially and politically—the reconstruction of an historic Armenian church in the center of town.

The town has built a memorial to the victims of 1915. And Kurdish leaders here have generally expressed their sympathy for the conditions endured by the Armenian community.

For a traveler who is arriving at Diyarbakir, perhaps the first visible sign of this new attitude is a road sign that welcomes visitors to Diyarbakir. The sign is written in Kurdish, Turkish, and in Armenian. The Armenian phrase for welcome, *bari ekak*, is prominently centered. The phrase is written twice, as if it was being shouted by a welcoming host.

The Four Tigranakerts

The ancient Armenian city of Tigranakert that is associated with the modern city of Diyarbakir is one of four cities that were founded by Tigran the Great. The other Tigranakerts were located in Nakhichevan, Utik, and in Artsakh.

Of these four Tigranakerts, only the Tigranakert of Artsakh has been excavated for study by archaeologists. This city is located near Askeran, just north of Stepanakert. The excavations reveal that the Tigranakert of Artsakh was an Armenian city two millennia ago.

The Tigranakert of Utik is located east of Artsakh, in today's Republic of Azerbaijan. The location of the Tigranakert of Nakhichevan has been lost to history.

HIGHLIGHTS OF DIYARBAKIR

At the center of the walled city of Diyarbakir, the historic Armenian **Cathedral of Soorp Giragos** is the single greatest pilgrimage site for Armenians. The monument is significant both for its role in the history of the Armenian Church, and also during the calamity of 1915.

The bell tower of Soorp Giragos was said to be the tallest structure in Diyarbakir until 1915, when the Turkish Army, intent on destroying a symbol of the Armenian community, felled it with cannon fire. The damage to Soorp Giragos was repaired almost a century later. The bell tower was rebuilt, and the restoration of the church was completed, in 2012.

The ruins of **Soorp Sarkis**, which are also within the walled city and are just a short walk from Soorp Giragos, are also sought out by visitors in search of Diyarbakir's Armenian past.

The greatest highlights of the region of Diyarbakir lie north of the city in **Palu** and in **Chunkush**. Palu is the site of the famous Church of **Soorp Grigor Lusavorich (St. Gregory the Illuminator)** and of nearby caves where Mesrop Mashtots is believed to have labored on the creation of the Armenian alphabet.

VISITING DIYARBAKIR TODAY

The church of **Soorp Giragos** is the most compelling site in the city of Diyarbakir for Armenian pilgrims. The recent reconstruction and resurrection of this church—which is the largest Armenian church in the region and perhaps in all of the Middle East—symbolizes to many the hope of a better future for the Armenian community of today's Turkey.

The Armenians of Diyarbakir constructed the original church of Soorp Giragos in 1518, and performed renovations and additions about a century later. The building fell into disrepair after 1915, and a restoration was begun in 2010. The building is located in the Sur district of Diyarbakir, a neighborhood that was densely populated with Armenians until one century ago.

Soorp Giragos is noteworthy for its exterior design, which is a dramatic departure from typical Armenian architecture. The building has a flat roof and lacks the drum and conical dome that is common to Armenian churches. Soorp Giragos does have a bell tower, but even the architecture of this tower is a departure from traditional Armenian styles. The tower is narrow and several stories tall.

Christina Maranci, the scholar of Armenian art and architecture, compares the design of the bell tower to the many minarets of Diyarbakir. According to Maranci, "with its prominent position on the horizon, the tower must have made an aggressive statement about the presence of an Armenian community in Amida/Diarbekir [Diyarbakir]."

The original bell tower of Soorp Giragos was reputed to be the tallest structure in Diyarbakir when it was built. The tower has today lost this distinction, but it is still one of the tallest structures within the old walled city.

Today's tower is the third that has graced Soorp Giragos over the years. The original tower of 1882—then one of the tallest structures in the city—was topped by an onion dome but was replaced 31 years later, soon after it had been damaged in a storm. The replacement tower, a neo-Gothic style structure, featured a clock, in addition to a bell and was even taller than the original. This tower was allowed to stand for just two years. The Turkish army destroyed it in 1915.

The rest of the church was not destroyed in 1915, but it began to fall into disrepair in the 1950s. By the 1990s, the timbers of the roof had collapsed, and only the walls of the church remained. The roof was replaced in 2010 as part of an extensive reconstruction of the site. A new tower, the third in the life of the church, was also built. This tower again features an onion dome, and again, no clock. Reconstruction was completed, and the church was reopened, in 2012.

The interior of Soorp Giragos is also noteworthy, and features a design of numerous arches and seven altars. There's nothing modest about this church. The sanctuary has a balcony, and can accommodate about 2,500 parishioners.

The reconstruction of Soorp Giragos was organized locally by Diyarbakir's **Soorp Giragos Armenian Church Foundation**. The project was funded by contributions from *Tigranakertsis* and other Armenians throughout the world. The local Kurdish government, the Diyarbakir Metropolitan Municipality, also provided significant financial support to the reconstruction.

The ruins of Soorp Sarkis are also located within the city walls of Diyarbakir. **Soorp Sarkis** is believed to have been built during the sixteenth century, in the same era as the construction of Soorp Giragos. The ruins have no roof, and are similar to the appearance of Soorp Giragos prior to its recent reconstruction.

Soorp Sarkis is located near the **Mardin Gate**, which is located on the city's south side. The church stands behind a tall wall on the Ali Pasa Street. When I visited the church in 2014, I gained access by climbing through a small hole near the bottom of one of the perimeter walls—an undignified manner of entry, to be sure.

The altars of Soorp Giragos

THE LAST ARMENIANS OF DIYARBAKIR

Some thirty years ago in Diyarbakir, the priest of the town's last Armenian church, *Soorp Giragos*, had just left town. The church was shuttered. The school's blackboards were folded and put away for the last time. The Armenian community of Diyarbakir had become so greatly diminished that there was no flock for a priest, no students for a teacher.

And there was no home for **Sarkis** and **Baydzar**, two of the last Armenians who still lived in town.

So, back in 1984, the couple was invited to make a home for themselves at the **Mother Mary Assyrian Church** in Diyarbakir. Their small apartment on the church campus became a refuge in a city that was, mostly, hostile to Armenians.

Baydzar had moved to Diyarbakir in 1950 when she married Sarkis. Together, they had made Diyarbakir their home for all of their married life together, even as Armenians around them left town for safer areas, more hospitable areas, areas such as Istanbul. Or America.

Baydzar and Sarkis became known to many as the **Last Armenians of Diyarbakir**. They aren't really the last. There are other Armenians who stayed, and who still live in the region today.

But Baydzar and Sarkis became known as the Last Armenians because of their resilience. They stayed when so many others left, and they didn't always keep their identity a secret. They were the hidden Armenians who refused to hide.

The couple was celebrated in newspapers in April 2014 when they renewed their wedding vows at a civil ceremony in Diyarbakir. The mayor of Diyarbakir was one of the official witnesses. Some media referred to them as newly-weds, as if they were octogenarians who were exchanging wedding vows for the first time. This wasn't true.

Perhaps the confusion was caused by the type of wedding ceremony that had been performed for them 64 years earlier. Baydzar and Sarkis had exchanged vows in a small room *adjoining* the Soorp Giragos Armenian church.

Baydzar and Sarkis were both Christian Armenians, but the identity papers of Sarkis erroneously identified him as a Muslim. Sarkis couldn't marry Baydzar in the church! After more than one half century, Sarkis straightened out the paper work, and they were able to exchange vows in church.

I met Baydzar and Sarkis at their home in Diyarbakir in 2014, shortly after their wedding. We communicated through a translator who understood her unusual blend of Turkish, Kurdish, and Armenian.

She showed me old photographs of her family. She talked about life in Diyarbakir.

I learned that her parents had been saved from death in 1915 when an Alevi family gave them refuge in a village in Diyarbakir province.

We visited for a bit beside the Rose Garden of her small apartment. Before Baydzar could grow weary of our visit, or at least before she had the opportunity to complain of growing weary, we wished her well and said goodbye.

One month later, the newspapers that had just so recently written about Baydzar's wedding, were now writing about Baydzar again.

Baydzar passed away on June 23, 2014, just one month after our chat in the Rose Garden. She was 87 years old and was eulogized as one of the last Armenians of Diyarbakir. She is buried in Dyarbakir's Armenian cemetery.

In recent years, this neighborhood has become plagued by crime, particularly by pickpocketing, at all hours of day and evening. There's no need to avoid this area, but travelers should be alert and should never walk alone on the streets and alleys near Soorp Sarkis.

An **Armenian cemetery** is located about 100 meters from **Urfa Gate**, which is located on the city's west side. The municipality constructed a wall around the cemetery during the 1990s to protect it from vandalism and plunder, but by the time the wall was built, extensive damage had already been done. This is the cemetery where Baydzar, one of the last Armenians of Diyarbakir, is buried.

You can reach the cemetery by leaving Diyarbakir through the Urfa Gate. After passing through the gate, turn left and walk one block, then turn right and walk 100 meters.

During the renovation of Soorp Giragos, the deeds for some 200 parcels of property were discovered buried beneath the floor of the church. The deeds indicated that the Armenian Church had owned much of the land surrounding this cemetery until 1915.

Outside the walled city, in the south of Diyarbakir, the municipality in 2013 erected a memorial, known as the **Monument of Common Conscience**, which honors the perished Armenians, as well as other groups that were subjected to massacres in these lands. The word genocide is not used, but the suffering of the Armenians is commemorated. This is the first and only monument in Western Armenia, today's eastern provinces of Turkey, that openly commemorates the suffering of the Armenians.

The monument's inscription appears in Turkish, Kurdish, Arabic, Armenian, Hebrew, and English. The English version states, perhaps inelegantly, "We shared the pains so that they are not suffered again." A more polished translation into English would have been "We share the pain so that it is not repeated."

The mayor of Diyarbakir spoke at the dedication of the monument in 2013. He is quoted by the US-based *Armenian Weekly* newspaper as saying "We Kurds, in the name of our ancestors, apologize for the massacres and deportations of the Armenians and Assyrians in 1915."

The statement suggested an official Kurdish interest in reconciliation, at least at this local level. The monument had already fallen into disrepair by the end of the 2014.

Bari Ekak (Welcome!)

Ruins of Soorp Sarkis

The **City Walls of Diyarbakir**, themselves, are noteworthy, and were constructed with 72 towers, 12 buttresses, and four large iron gates. The local Christian tradition attributes a religious symbolism to the components of the wall. The 72 towers signify the 72 disciples of Jesus. Twelve buttresses represent the 12 Apostles. And the four gates connote the four gospels of the New Testament.

The **Dicle Bridge**—the thousand year old bridge that spans the Tigris River just south of the city—is perhaps the most iconic symbol of Diyarbakir. The bridge is also known as the Silvan Bridge because it leads to Silvan, but many locals simply call it The Bridge, without generating any confusion. There is no other bridge in Diyarbakir that competes with its grandeur and beauty.

This famous bridge was completed in AD 1065, and features a graceful stone design of ten arches. To reach the bridge, exit the city from the **Mardin Gate**, which is at the south, and continue south for about three kilometers.

The site has become a pedestrian haven—and a popular site for wedding photos— ever since 2009 when motor vehicles were banned and directed to a new bridge farther south.

THE LAST 100 YEARS AT SOORP GIRAGOS

The destruction of the Soorp Giragos bell tower in 1915 marked the beginning of a century of decline, and ultimately of rebirth, for the physical structure of this church.

The government seized the church sometime after 1915, and the building was used as a military headquarters during World War I, and then as a warehouse until sometime in the 1950s.

By the 1960s, ownership of the church had been restored to the Armenian community, and the site was again used as a church until 1983.

A priest had been in residence at Soorp Giragos and there had been an Armenian school there, too. But by 1983 the Armenian community had withered. The school closed. The priest left.

During a recent visit to Soorp Giragos, I met an Armenian man named Behcet. He had been born in a nearby village, and he moved to Diyarbakir in 1981. He told me what he recalled about the recent history of the church, and of the Armenian community. After the priest left in 1983, things started to fall apart, he said.

Portraits of the Tigranakertsi of 1914, on display at Soorp Giragos

Memorial to the Armenians

"Nobody was here. The place was abandoned. We had a lot of difficulties both from the state and the local population."

Behcet recalled sitting in the church courtyard back in 1982 and 1983, talking with the priest before his departure. We couldn't even say we were Armenian, he told me, but still, "at no point did we run away from being Armenian."

By the 1990s, the timbers of the roof had collapsed and Soorp Giragos was opened to the sky. Restoration was begun in 2010 and the church reopened two years later.

FUNCTIONING ARMENIAN CHURCHES

There were approximately 2,300 functioning Armenian churches Ottoman Turkey in 1915. In today's Turkey, which is the successor state of the Ottoman Empire, there are fewer than 50. Most of these churches are located in Istanbul. Almost all of the rest have been destroyed since 1915, or have fallen to ruins.

Soorp Giragos in Dyarbakir is today one of the few Armenian churches outside of Istanbul that has survived.

This is also the largest and most prominent functioning Armenian church in Turkey's eastern provinces, a region that is known to Armenians as Western Armenia. Soorp Giragos operates as a church, serves a small local Armenian community, and regularly performs the *badarak*, or Divine Liturgy.

Other Armenian churches in Western Armenia also function, or exist, but by varying degrees.

For example, the *badarak* is performed once each year at Soorp Khatch (the Church of the Holy Cross) on Aghtamar Island, but this church was seized by the Turkish authorities and is operated by the state as a museum. It does not serve a local community. The *badarak* is performed, but only with permission of the government. Thus, this cannot be counted as a functioning Armenian church.

100 YEARS AGO ARMENIANS HAD 2,300 FUNCTIONING CHURCHES HERE. TODAY THEY HAVE FEWER THAN 50

The property of Varagavank, near the city of Van, is maintained by Armenians, but it serves no local community and the deed to the property is supposedly held by the descendant of a Turk who acquired title after 1915, and not by the Armenian Church. Religious services are not performed at the church. This church, also, cannot be characterized as functioning.

An Armenian church functions in Kayseri, which is located in Cappadocia, just west of Western Armenia. And numerous churches—local sources in Istanbul say there are 36 of them—function, perform the *badarak*, and serve the Armenian community of greater Istanbul, which is also outside of historic Western Armenia

THE REGION OF DIYARBAKIR

Chunkush

Chunkush is an historically Armenian region that is located in the northern sector of the province of Diyarbakir. The name of the town appears as Cungus on Turkish maps. Pilgrims will find it easy to visit this area as part of a trip from either the city of Diyarbakir, or from **Kharpert** (known in Turkey today as **Harpoot**).

One of the most important surviving Armenian monuments in Chunkush is the church of **Soorp Garabed**. Even in ruins today, the building is impressive, and attests to the wealth and prominence of the Armenians here.

The ruins of an Armenian Catholic church are located on a hill overlooking Soorp Garabed. Only one wall remains of the Catholic church. The US-based *Armenian Weekly* newspaper has documented considerable damage that has been suffered by this church since 2012. At the current rate of destruction, it is likely that all traces of this church will soon be gone.

To get there, travel about 40 kilometers south of Elazig and Kharpert. **GPS map coordinates** for Soorp Garabed, in Chunkush: 38° 12' 35.57" N 39° 17' 8.73" E

Former Armenian Quarter of Chunkush

Chunkush is also the site of an Armenian monastery that is known as **Sirahayats**. The surviving church of this monastery, **Soorp Astvatsatsin**, is located near the home of the oldest surviving Armenian of Chunkush, a woman named Asiya (pronounced *Ah-see-ah*). The English translation of the name of the Sirahayats monastery is "the monastery that looks out lovingly."

To get there, travel just east of the center of Chunkush. **GPS map coordinates** for Soorp Astvatsatsin, in Chunkush: 38° 12' 47.36" N 39° 17' 47.74" E

Dudan Gorge

The **Dudan Gorge** is a deep crevice located in a village named Yenikoy. The village is just outside Chunkush, and the gorge is known today by the Turkish name *Yudan Dere*. Stare down into the gorge, which is a fissure in the bedrock of the earth, and you cannot see the bottom. The gorge drops vertically to an unseen depth.

This gorge was a notorious killing zone in 1915.

During the "deportations" of 1915, this was the relocation site for the entire Armenian population of Chunkush. Upon their arrival here, they were herded into the chasm by bayonets and clubs, or they were killed and then pushed into the ravine. Rappel down into the ravine today, if you can, and you'll find yourself deep inside a century-old grave of 10,000 victims.

This site is sacred but it's not secret. Dudan is well known as a killing zone, even by today's residents of the area, people who were born long after 1915.

During my visit to the site, I encountered two teenage girls who were hiking nearby. Speaking in Turkish through a translator, they told me what they knew about Dudan: "When the Armenians were fighting, this is where they fell in," one of them said.

The girl made the statement so matter-of-factly, that I concluded it was something she must have been taught in school. This was part of her local history. This, the place where ten thousand Armenians fell.

The Dudan Gorge,
sacred grave of 10,000 Armenians

If this is indeed something that the local children learn in school—that Armenians fell into the gorge in 1915—then one imagines them glancing out their classroom window during this lesson and looking down into the gorge. In 2014 a three-story elementary school was built about 100 meters from the gorge, and now towers above it.

To get there, travel about 10 kilometers east of Chunkush. **GPS map coordinates** for Dudan Gorge: 38° 10' 57.45"N 39° 24' 16.57" E

Palu

Palu was a densely populated region of about 40 Armenian villages until 1915, and was the site of the monasteries of Gevorg of Palu and Mesrop of Palu. Today, the ruins of an Urartian fortress remain on a mountain peak that towers above the ruins of the **Soorp Lusavorich** church.

Near the hilltop fortress are caves that are said to have been used by **Mesrop Mashtots** while he was creating the Armenian alphabet. The connection to Mashtots is just a legend, and there's no conclusive evidence linking him to this site. View Soorp Lusavorich from the mountaintop, and then drive to the bottom to fully explore its ruins.

After his visit to the region in 1893, H. F. B. Lynch described Palu as a "thriving borough" with about 2,000 houses and a population of between 10,000 and 12,000 people.

To get there, travel about 50 kilometers east of Elazig. **GPS map coordinates** for Soorp Grigor Lusavorich, in Palu: 38° 41' 56.86" N 39° 57' 21.11" E

Soorp Lusavorich, in Palu

THE OLDEST ARMENIAN OF CHUNKUSH

The village of Chunkush was home to about 10,000 Armenians, and hardly anyone else, until 1915.

That's when the Armenians were driven out, and were marched for two hours to a ravine known as the **Dudan Gorge**. Once they arrived at the ravine, they were herded by the force of batons and bayonets into its depths. Here they died, if they hadn't already perished before entering the abyss.

One young Armenian girl, not more than ten years of age, stood at the edge of death. She was part of a group that had been marched to the ravine on one of the killing days—the day on which her Chunkush neighborhood had been selected for this "deportation."

This girl was pretty, and she must have captured the attention of one of the Turkish soldiers who were herding the Armenians to their deaths. Her life was spared. At the age of ten, she became the soldier's bride.

Five years later, in 1920, a baby was born from their union. This baby, named Asiya, was raised in Chunkush by her mother, a genocide survivor who had been able to remain in the home of her husband as one of the village's hidden Armenians.

When I met Asiya in 2014, she was the oldest surviving Armenian, and indeed, the only Armenian, of Chunkush. Speaking through a translator, Asiya told me her story.

Her father, the Turkish solder, had died when Asiya was three or four years old. While Asiya was growing up, Asiya's mother had taught her that she was an Armenian child. Her mother also taught her that her identity as an Armenian was information that they could not share with the neighbors. Their identity had to remain hidden.

I asked Asiya about the massacres of 1915. Her mother must have explained to her what had happened. But Asiya refused to talk about it.

Asiya was about 95 years old when I met her in 2014. Her life has been swept along in a torrent of sadness. I asked her how she feels when, as the only Armenian of Chunkush, she meets Armenian visitors from the Diaspora.

"I get happy as much as a mountain," she told me.

Bitlis

INTRODUCTION

The region of **Bitlis** includes the towns of **Bitlis**, **Mush**, and **Sasun**, each of which figures prominently in Armenian history.

This part of historic Western Armenia is believed to have been one of the earliest centers of Armenian settlement. The Greek geographer Strabo, writing in the first century, refers to Armenians as having been in this region as early as the second century BC.

The Bitlis region was incorporated into the Ottoman Empire in 1512, by which time Bitlis was home to several Armenian churches and monasteries, and had already become a center for Armenian manuscript production.

By 1915 the city of Bitlis had become the provincial capital, with a population of about 30,000, of whom one third were Armenian. At about the same time, it is estimated that about 70,000 Armenians lived in the 120 villages and towns throughout the Mush Valley.

Bitlis was situated on a major trade route that connected the Armenian Plateau with Mesopotamia. Bitlis was also a location of strategic military importance for this reason.

The town of Mush, by contrast, was more isolated, and less important for trade, but was no less a center for Armenian life. Thousands of manuscripts were copied at Mush, many of which survived the genocide and are preserved in Yerevan at the Matenadaran.

Among the most famous of the surviving manuscripts are those that comprise a holy book known as the **Homilies of Mush**.

Sasun is remembered in contemporary history for its uprisings against misrule beginning in 1894 and for the support that the *Sasuntsis* rendered in defense of Armenians from other parts of the Ottoman Empire during the genocide.

The people of Sasun, particularly the men, are also remembered as sojourners, or *pandukhts*, who left Sasun to earn money which they then used to aid their families in Sasun, as well as to assist other Armenians in need during the genocide.

Perhaps the most renowned *pandukht* of Sasun during the modern era was **Kevork Chavush**. This freedom fighter left Sasun, as did so many *pandukhts*, to earn money in Aleppo. After spending the year of 1889 away from Sasun, he returned to help defend his fellow villagers.

VISITING THE BITLIS REGION TODAY

A group of *khatchkars* in the village of **Por**, which is just outside Bitlis, are among the world's largest examples of this art form. This is also certainly one of the most significant collections of *khatchkars* in today's Turkey.

The engraved stone crosses at Por date back to the fourteenth and fifteenth centuries and are associated with the nearby Soorp Anania Armenian Church and with an Armenian monastery from that period. The *khatchkars* depict birds and fish, which is unusual for this Armenian art form.

The Turkish name for the village of Por is **Degirmenalti**. The village is located about seven kilometers northeast of Bitlis.

For the best photography, plan to be at Por in late afternoon. *Khatchkars* are inscribed on the side that faces west, so if you arrive late in the day you can photograph the inscribed side of the *khatchkars*, illuminated by the late day sun.

To get there, travel about eight kilometers north of Bitlis. **GPS map coordinates** for Soorp Anania and the *khatchkars*, in the village of Por: 38° 25' 48.84" N 42° 10' 31.15" E

Arakelots, the Monastery of the Holy Apostle, dates back to the tenth century and is certainly the greatest Armenian site of Mush. Today the once-beautiful site is reduced to ruins, but enough of the monument remains to make a trip here rewarding.

Arakelots, the Monastery of the Holy Apostles in Mush, c. 1915.
The site was destroyed in the 1960s.
Photo by Vartan A. Hampikian, Courtesy of John Donelian

A church at Arakelots is believed to have been founded by St. Gregory the Illuminator in the fourth century, several centuries before the establishment of the monastery. None of the ruins now present can be dated to that era, however.

It is said that St. Gregory used an original building at this site to house relics of Saints Peter and Paul, and of the Apostle Andrew, which he received from Rome. The "relics" included the arms (the actual arms!) of Peter, Paul, and Andrew.

When it was intact, the complex consisted of a main church, two chapels, a gavit or meeting room, and a bell tower. The main church had been constructed from brick, which is a departure from the norm for Armenian churches, for which hewn stone is the more common building material.

Arakelots was attacked and plundered of its treasures in 1915, but its main church and chapels were reported to have remained in good structural condition until 1960. A government official from Mush used dynamite to destroy the ancient structures sometime after 1960.

Before the plunder, the illuminated manuscripts known as the **Homilies of Mush** had been preserved at Arakelots. A homily is a book containing sermons, and the Homilies of Mush were a grand, oversized book, containing hundreds of pages of illuminated manuscripts that had been created sometime around the year 1200.

The manuscripts were saved by two women who carried them to safety across the Russian frontier to Yerevan. They are now preserved at the Matenadaran, Armenia's famous manuscript repository, in Yerevan.

A wooden door from Arakelots has survived the destruction, and is on display at the National Museum in Yerevan. In 1916, a year after the monastery had been looted and abandoned, an Armenian had discovered the door in Bitlis and carried it to Tbilisi for safekeeping. In 1925 the door was transferred to Yerevan.

To get there, travel east on the main road just past the bus station of Mush until you see a sign indicating the end of Mush, and a nearby sign for "Arek Kilise," which is the Turkish name for Arakelots. The monastery is eight kilometers from the turnoff, on a road that starts fine, and then degenerates to unpaved trail just past the last village.

For this trek it's best to use a 4WD vehicle with a high suspension, and then plan to hike the last stretch. The hike to the ruins should take about 90 minutes. **GPS map coordinates** for Arakelots: 38 41' 45" N, 41 31' 10" E

Soorp Garabed is another highlight of the Mush region, and was located on a mountain slope about 35 kilometers northwest of town in the Kurdish village of Chengelli. Soorp Garabed (Soorp Karapet, or St. Charles) was destroyed by the Turks sometime after the genocide, and there is today very little here to view. The monastery was founded in the fourth century, by St. Gregory the

Illuminator, making it a contemporary of Soorp Arakelots, which was founded at the same time by the same patriarch, and which has also been largely destroyed.

Soorp Garabed boasts a strong connection to **Mkrtich Khrimian**, also known as Khrimian Hayrig. In the nineteenth century, **Khrimian Hayrig** had become the prelate of Mush. He established a printing press and a school at Soorp Garabed, and he published a journal, the **Eagle of Taron**.

H. F. B. Lynch traveled to Soorp Garabed in 1893, and wrote at length about the site in his famous book *Armenia: Travels and Studies*. By the time of his visit, wrote Lynch, "this once flourishing monastery has been stripped of much of its glamour…. The library was pillaged by Kurds during the first half of the present century [the 1800s], and its contents burnt or littered about the courts."

Soorp Garabed, in the Mush region, c. 1915.
The monastery was destroyed shortly afterward.
Photo by Vartan A. Hampikian, Courtesy of John Donelian

The city and fortress of Bitlis, c. 1915.
This image was printed several years later, in 1923.
Photo by Vartan A. Hampikian, Courtesy of John Donelian

Soorp Garabed is today almost entirely destroyed, but it is still a site of pilgrimage for many Armenians. This monastery is also known by the names St. John the Baptist, or Soorp Hovhannes Mkrtich. Muslims had referred to the site as *Chengelli Kelise*, the Church of the Bells.

The historian Robert H. Hewsen reports that the monastery earned this name "because by special dispensation it alone was allowed to ring bells, a privilege normally denied to churches in the Ottoman Empire." Lynch, too, acknowledged that the site was known as Chengelli because its bells were heard in the plains from afar.

To get there, travel 35 kilometers northeast of Mush. **GPS map coordinates** for Soorp Garabed: 38 57' 42" N, 41 11' 30" E

The ruins of two interesting churches are located east of **Tatvan**, on the shore of Lake Van but within the region of Bitlis. Soorp **Sarkis (St. Sarkis Church)** is located in the village that is today known as **Hanelmali Village**, but which may be more familiar to Armenians by the earlier Armenian name Khunjorgin. This village is located immediately east of Tatvan. From the hilltop on which Soorp Sarkis is built one can enjoy a clear view of nearby Tatvan.

The village of **Soorp** is located on a bluff that towers above the shore of Lake Van. Soorp is still within the region of Bitlis, a bit farther east from Hanelmali, and is today known by its Turkish name **Yelkenli**. The village is home to the **Soorp Hovhannes Church**, which is today in poor but largely intact condition.

To get there, travel east from Tatvan along the shore of Lake Van to view both churches. **GPS map coordinates** for Soorp Sarkis at the village of Hanelmali (former Armenian village of Khunjorgin): 38° 28' 51.83" N 42° 20' 7.96" E. **GPS map coordinates** for Soorp Hovhannes Church at the village of Yelkenli (former Armenian village of Soorp): 38° 29' 38.99" N 42° 32'48.92" E

H. F. B. Lynch visited Soorp in 1893, and described it as having fertile fields, a little bay of U-shaped curvature, and a mixed population of Armenians and Moslems.

LOOKING FOR BURIED TREASURE

I was in Mush searching for the location of the ruins of Arakelots when I stopped to ask directions. I stopped three, maybe four, times. At each stop, my inquiry prompted the same reply. You're looking for the gold?

Many of the people who live in the villages near Armenian monuments assume that if someone is traveling all the way to the ruins of an old Armenian monastery, then the person must be looking for the buried treasure that is supposedly hidden at every Armenian church in Western Armenia.

At countless churches that I visited, not just in Mush, but everywhere in Western Armenia, the areas beneath altars had been excavated. The floors near the entryways had been dug up.

If anyone *really* hid any treasure beneath these Armenian churches and monasteries one century ago, then the treasures must certainly have been removed by now. The continued excavations damage the foundations of these buildings, and thus threaten the survival of the real treasures, which are the monuments themselves.

Khatchkars in the village of Pors, near Bitlis
Photo by Samvel Karapetyan, Courtesy of Research on Armenian Architecture Foundation

Erzerum

Erzerum is located at the center of the Armenian Plateau and constituted a region known historically to Armenians as **Bardzar Hayk—Upper Armenia**. The region's capital city of Erzerum was historically known to Armenians as **Karin**.

There is today little physical evidence of the rich history of the Armenians in Erzerum. For much of the past century, the region has been cleared of any relics and monuments that would support the claim that this land had ever been Armenian. Even the local museum, the **Erzerum Archaeological Museum**, has no Armenian artifacts on display.

During the centuries before the physical evidence had been cleared away, the Armenians themselves were removed from the province. For hundreds of years during the period of Ottoman rule, officially sanctioned persecution was used as a means of de-Armenianizing the region, and of de-Armenianizing the Armenian people themselves.

De-Armenianization is explained by Ashot A. Melkonyan, the scholar of Armenian history and an expert on Ottoman demography. Melkonyan concludes that Erzerum, *Bardzar Hayk* (Upper Armenia) and Western Armenia "was ethnically cleansed over a long period through the intentional policies of forced conversion [to Islam], assimilation, massacre, and expulsion."

Some of the Armenians who had been forced to convert to Islam became known as the *kes-kes*, or the half-and-half. These Armenians were outwardly Turkish and supposedly were adherents of Islam. But privately they identified as Armenian.

Erzinjan (Erzincan) was the second largest city of Erzerum province, and just prior to 1915 it had a population of about 25,000, of whom half were Armenian. Erzinjan was located in a seismically active area, on a fault line, 175 kilometers west of Erzerum.

After a devastating quake in 1939, the city was rebuilt in a new location nearby, this time with wide avenues and large plazas. There's nothing ancient to view here today.

West of Erzinjan in the tiny village of **Dogan** there is an old Armenian church in an old village that was, until 1915, Armenian, as well. This church formed part of the **Monastery of Nine Tombs**, and was the fourth century burial place for King Trdat III and Queen Ashkhen, and seven other saints. This is one of a handful of relics of Armenia that still exist in remote locations in Erzerum province.

This tiny and remote village is located north of **Kemah**, which is notorious as the site of the **Kemah Gorge**. In 1915, the perpetrators of the genocide killed as many as 25,000 Armenian deportees from throughout the Erzinjan region by pushing them or otherwise forcing them to fall from the top of the cliff into the Euphrates River below.

The **Monastery of Aparank**, also known as the **Monastery of Soorp Grigor (St. Gregory) of Aparank**, may be the most significant Armenian monument that is still standing in Erzerum province today. The site includes a pair of giant *khatchkars* that each measure about six meters tall, and which date to the late twelfth century.

Ruins of a home in western Erzerum

Aparank is located about 15 kilometers southwest of **Tercan**, which is the only significant town midway between Erzinjan and Erzerum. The monastery and the *khatchkars* are located on a hill-top. Allow 45 minutes for the three-kilometer hike.

GETTING TO DIYARBAKIR AND BITLIS

There are several flights to Diyarbakir each day from Istanbul and Ankara. There is no airport at Bitlis. Instead, fly into Mush, and make a combined visit of Bitlis and Mush. There are several flights to Mush each day from Istanbul, and there is frequent bus service between Mush and Bitlis. Bitlis and Mush are reached conveniently by bus from Van, Diyarbakir, and Erzerum.

When to Visit

The *badarak* is performed on most Sundays at the Soorp Giragos Church in Diyarbakir, so plan to be in town on a Sunday morning.

Suggested Itinerary

This suggested itinerary covers the highlights of the Diyarbakir, Bitlis, and Erzerum regions, in roughly the order of significance of the sites, so that you can plan a visit of from one to four days.

1. Day One: Morning at the ruins of Soorp Arakelots, near Mush (half day) and then afternoon at the khatchkars in the village of Por, near Bitlis (half day).

2. Day Two: Diyarbakir church of Soorp Giragos, and south of the city at the Dicle Bridge over the Tigris River.

3. Day Three: The churches of Palu and Chunkush, in the northern sector of Diyarbakir province, not far from Kharpert.

4. Day Four: Traveling to Erzerum is time-consuming, and will not lead to many sites of interest to most Armenian pilgrims. Visit Aparank, near the town of Tercan, and the village of Dogan, as part of a journey heading to (or from) Kars.

The Monastery of the Nine Tombs
in the western Erzerum village of Dogan

Kharpert and Sebastia

The Monastery of Khulavank, near Kharpert

SIVAS

DIVRIGHI

Ortajimen Hill
2270 / 7447

Great Golbashi
3250 / 10663

Munzur

HAIDARI / KIZILKILISE
(GARMIR VANK)

S. Krikor
Lusaworich

Navril (Narvid)

Baratsor

(Aghzunik)   (Anakom)

ZERNAG
(MNTSUR)

Ovajik

Hinzori
(Khntsor)

Viko (Okho)   (Tashd)

Herdif (Hardiw)

Aregi

Egin

Munzur
3188 / 10459

Balikan
(Khach'achur)
2150 / 7054

Pardi

TUZHIK

Payizagan (P'aydagan)

Jivarik (Tsuarij)

Kizilkilise

Armutak
(Armět'agh)

Bizmishen
(Pazmashēn)

EGIN
(AKN)

Hinsor (Khntsor)

BARASOR
(BARATSOR)

SANJAK

Pokir (P'ok'r)
2300 / 7546

Sin

Holhol
(Kholkholk)

Gemirgap (Kamrkab)

Vardenig

Desht
(Tashd)

Halvuri (Halvori)

S. Garabed of
Halvori

Kortan Kom
(Khordan Kom)

Pegir (Perga)

Sabos

S. Kevork

Asbutka
(Anchnti)

of

Mazgirt

PAH (PAKH)

Pah

Jukur (Chashadur)

Hopik (Khobag)

S. T'oros

S. Kevork

S. Hagop

HOZAT
(Lusatarich)

Kibris Kom

(Khozn Kegh)

Husiki vank

(Geghpaghnik)

S. Sarkis

CHEMISHGEZEK
(CH'MSHGADZAK)

Tavuk
(T'ukh)

MAZGIRT
(METZGERD)

ARAPKIR

(Vardenig)

DERSIM

Hulman
(Khulmin)

Shotig (Shepig)

S. Eghia

Savukh

Charsanjak

(Shikh)

Akkilise
(Abivank)

Hasan Chelebi

Anberge (Ambrga)

S. Asduatzamayr

Aghin
(Aghi)

(Lower
Vardenig)

(Suchag)

Köderich (Geterich')

S. Asduatzatzin

(Vank)

Vaskovan (Vosgevan)

(Şaghman)

(T'il)

Hekim Han

Pulur
(Plur)

Murat

Aratzani

Sakaltutan

Pashaghak
(Pashavank')

Paghnig

PERI / CHARSANJAK (P'ERIN)

(Goghpenig)

Hersenk (Harsenig)

Pertek (Pertag)

Vasgert
(Vazgérd)

Peri

(Arkavan)

KEBAN MADEN
(HAVU)

(K'ĕawrp'ĕ)

Murati

(Ayvoz)

Orik (Urig / Ureg)

GÜRÜN

Keban

(Ērzrug)

Ma

Maden

(Khulakiugh)

Harput (Kharpert)

Mezraa
(Mēzirē)

HARPUT (KHARPERT)
(Hiusenig)

(Alashgerd)

PALU

Mushovka
(Mishavga)

(Pazmashēn)

Akcha-Dagh

Hamara

Tatmavank' S. Asdvatzatzin

Kesrik (K'ěsirig)
(Parchanj)

(Mōrenig)

(Mughē)

(Alishan)

(Ich'mě)

DARENDE

(Mushar)

Kiakka

[Mshar]

Paghnik

Tatem
(Ballija)

(Vartat'il)

(Haŗig)

(Komk')

Euphrates

Tohma

[Arshamashat]

Masdar (Mastara)
2140 / 7021

S. Aharon

(Lower Khōkh)

(Shnt'il)

(T'lants'ig)

Karmri

AKCHA-DAGH
(Arka)

Anjar (Ansur /
Ansar)

Izoli

(Khanadaŗich)

S. Nshan

L. Goljuk
(L. Hazar)

(Chermukhd)

Old Malatya

(Upper Khōkh)

MALATYA

Orduzu (Eordeuoz)

Surek
(Tzovk' kiugh)

S. P'rgich (Shughr
Khandara)

Telek

Ergani (Western Tigris)

Kogh Lur

S. Lusaworich
(Shughr Khandara)

ERGANI
(ARGHANA)

SANJAK of MALATYA

Chunkush

CHERMIK
(CHERMUG)

Vilayet (Province) Capital

Sanjak (County) Capital

Kaza (District) Center

Harput   Ottoman Turkish Name (Official)

(Kharpert)   Western Armenian Name (Colloquial)

•   Armenian Village

Armenian Archbishop, Bishop, Prelate

Armenian Catholic Bishop

◆   Monastery

Lakape

KAHTA

Scale

0   25 mi

0   25 km

Pere

Adiyaman

HASANMANSUR

Courtesy of Robert H. Hewsen

Kharpert

INTRODUCTION

The province of **Kharpert** is the *Voski Dasht*, the Golden Plain, of the Armenian Plateau.

This area, which is the site of historic Armenian settlement of **Tsopk**, and which is known in today's Turkey as either Harpoot or Harput, is also one of the oldest areas of Armenian habitation. Some scholars believe that Kharpert may even be *the* cradle of the Armenian nation.

Whether the Armenian nation originated here, or farther east in Bitlis, or Van, or elsewhere, however, there is no dispute that Armenian Kharpert holds one of the keys to understanding the origins of the Armenian people.

In centuries past, Kharpert's fields of grain helped the region to earn its designation as the Golden Plain. By 1915, however, Kharpert had earned a new moniker: "the Slaughterhouse Province."

An American diplomat who lived in Kharpert from 1914 to 1917 bestowed the name upon the region. He selected the name after observing the fate of the deported Armenians who had been herded to Kharpert from their homes in other parts of the Armenian Plateau.

During the century before its demise in 1915, Armenian Kharpert had developed into a significant center for missionaries from the US, and for American-sponsored schools. The exposure of *Kharpertsi* Armenians (Armenians from Kharpert) to these US institutions in the late 1800s helped to inspire them to adopt

Western ways, and to travel to the US—sometimes as immigrants, and sometimes as sojourners or *pandukhts*, laborers who intended to work in the US, save their earnings, and then return to Kharpert to help their families.

Just prior to 1915, the top American diplomat in Kharpert had estimated that roughly 80 percent of the Armenians who immigrated to the United States had come from Kharpert.

These travelers formed some of the earliest Armenian communities in the United States, in the factory and mill towns of southern New England. Many settled in places such as Worcester, Massachusetts, which was the site in 1891 of the first Armenian church in the US.

Among Diaspora Armenians living in North America today, the *Kharpertsi* are believed to be among the most numerous. And for most of the twentieth century, say some, the Armenians of Kharpert were the quintessential Armenian Americans.

The old **Armenian Quarter** of Kharpert is now abandoned, and the hill beside the town's fortress, once packed with Armenian homes, is now just a grassy field. The pair of photographs on the following pages shows the contrast between 1915 and today.

The ruins of **Soorp Hagop** are still present on the hill, but they are unmarked, ignored, and destined for oblivion. Kharpert, itself, is also destined for oblivion without its Armenian population. In the region surrounding the town of Khapert, traces of the ruins of about 70 Armenian churches and monasteries still exist.

Fortress of Kharpert,
and the empty Armenian Quarter, 2014

HIGHLIGHTS OF KHARPERT REGION

The Golden Plain of Kharpert included such important Armenian areas as Malatya, Arabkir, and Egin (also known as Akn) in addition to the town of Kharpert from which the region takes its name.

In Kharpert, the Armenian sites of greatest interest today are the Fortress of Kharpert and the nearby ruins of the Monastery of Khulavank and the Monastery of Tadem. Pilgrims can readily visit each of these sites without the need for permits, and without hiking through difficult terrain. One can visit each of these sites in a single day-trip.

The hill beneath the Fortress of Kharpert holds the ruins of an Armenian church, and from this vista one can see the city of Elazig, formerly known as Mezre, a city that since the early 1800s has grown to replace Kharpert. Most visitors to Kharpert will find that it is a simple matter to use Elazig, and its modern hotels, as a base from which to travel.

Malatya, which is located west of Kharpert, is home to the Holy Trinity Armenian Church, which was undergoing reconstruction

Fortress of Kharpert, and the Armenian Quarter, c. 1914
Courtesy of Houshamadyan.org

in 2014. A handful of Armenians still live in Malatya, mostly in the neighborhood of this church. An historic Armenian cemetery is located nearby.

Mount Nemrut, known in Turkey as Nemrut Dagi, is a UNESCO World Heritage Site located a couple of hours' drive from Malatya. The site has an Armenian connection dating back to the first century BC through the Armenian King Antiochus I.

The Armenian towns of Chunkush and Palu are home to the ruins of significant Armenian monuments. These towns are close to Kharpert and can be conveniently visited as part of a trip to Kharpert. They are located in the region of Diyarbakir, however, and this book therefore includes them in the Diyarbakir chapter.

A BRIEF HISTORY OF KHARPERT

The origins of the Armenian people have been the subject of much research. In recent years ancient Greek sources have been re-examined and new archaeological and linguistic studies have shown that there may have been an Armenian presence in the lands of historic Armenia long before the first millennium BC.

This Armenian national identity originated on the lands that would later become known as the Armenian Plateau—the highlands that include Kharpert and Malatya. Richard G. Hovannisian, the scholar and professor of Armenian history at UCLA, concludes without ambiguity that "the emergence of a clearly identifiable Armenian ethnos took place on this highland." The importance of Kharpert and Malatya to Armenian national development has been reinforced in recent years by a growing body of evidence.

The Kharpert region had been part of Urartu, a kingdon populated by people who are widely recognized as the progenitors of the Armenians, until 585 BC. After Urartu fell, the area was controlled, briefly, in turns, by the Median Empire, the Persian Empire, and then by Alexander the Great.

The Armenian King Tigran the Great eventually annexed the region into Greater Armenia in 95 BC. This greatest of the great Armenian kings held his empire together for just forty years but the Armenians remained on the Armenian Plateau. They struggled. Sometimes they prospered. But mostly the Armenians persisted in maintaining their culture and faith.

This persistence in the face of foreign rule allowed the Armenians to maintain their separate ethnos through the millennia.

Arabs invaded Armenia in the mid-seventh century, and they controlled the Golden Plain of Kharpert for the next 300 years. The Byzantines took the region in the tenth century and were in turn driven out by the Seljuk Turks in the next century.

Turkmen tribes—contestants for control who were known colloquially as the Black Sheep and the White Sheep—disputed control of the region for some time thereafter.

The Ottomans put an end to the disputes, but the turmoil lingered. They took control of Kharpert in 1515 and ruled the Armenians for 400 years, until the cataclysm of 1915.

There were administrative border adjustments over the years, and by the end of the 1800s, Kharpert and Malatya had become joined in the same *vilayet* (province). The official name of this province became **Mamuret ul-Aziz**. The name was difficult to pronounce and so many in the region, and especially the Armenians, persisted in using the name Kharpert.

By the nineteenth century, the heart of the province had become located in the twin towns of Kharpert and Mezre. The town of Kharpert was situated atop a low mountain, at an elevation of about 1,450 meters, which is about 350 meters higher than the surrounding plain.

Mezre lay at the foot of this mountain, 350 meters below, and was the official administrative center of the region. Today Mezre is known as the city of **Elazig**. Throughout the 1900s, the population of Kharpert steadily declined, as its people relocated to Mezre.

This migration out of Kharpert and into Mezre was prompted mostly by the quest for convenience. Transportation was sometimes difficult within Kharpert in the winter because, at its higher elevation, the town's roads were often filled with snow. Communication and trade with the villages of the plain was easier from Mezre (Elazig) than from the heights of Kharpert, as well.

Kharpert and Mezre become widely known for the production of textiles, and especially for their production of fine silk cloth. A *Kharpertsi* named Krikor Ipekjian developed this industry. Ipekjian produced cloth of such fine quality that his goods were exempted from customs duties and taxes, and were granted other privileges from the government.

Ipekjian adopted the family name **Fabrikatorian**, which is the Armenian word, more or less, for factory owner. The Fabrikatorian

Vandalism at the Monastery of Tadem

family became a pillar of the community, and the Fabrikatorian name became known far beyond Kharpert. By the late 1800s, Fabrikatorian's five sons had all gone into the family business, and the business thrived, at least until 1915. The family—each of the sons, their wives, their children, and their mother—was killed that year. After 1915 there was no one left alive in Kharpert who knew how to operate the silk factory, and so it was abandoned.

Kharpert would become famous, for a time, as the home to the American Board of Commissioners for Foreign Missions operating in Turkey. The mission station included a theological seminary, a college, and an orphanage. As a result of the missionary work, an Armenian Protestant congregation had been established by 1856 in Kharpert.

The mission college was originally named **Armenia College** when it was incorporated in 1876. The name proved controversial with the Turkish authorities, and the college was compelled in 1888 to change its name to the less offensive **Euphrates College**.

Within four years of its incorporation, Armenia College had graduated a small class of men, and a group of women received degrees within another three years. Classes were taught in Armenian, but advanced students also received lectures in English, which proved helpful to so many of the students who pursued further studies at the American University of Beirut, or in the United States.

By 1898, Euphrates College had an enrollment of about 1,000 students. And throughout Kharpert there were 63 mission schools with almost 4,000 pupils. The schools, and their enrollments, attest to the remarkable success of the American missions here.

The presence of American missionaries in Kharpert in turn led to the need for a US diplomatic presence to represent their interests. By 1895, the US Congress had approved the establishment of a consulate in Kharpert, and also in Erzerum, which is located to the east. The massacres of 1895 prevented the posts from being filled, however. It would be another five years before there would be an official US diplomatic presence in Kharpert.

Motivated to protect US interests in the region, the United States finally staffed its consulate in Kharpert in 1900 with the arrival of US Consul Thomas H. Norton. Several consuls would serve during the course of the next 14 years, culminating with the appointment in May 1914 of **US Consul Leslie A. Davis**.

Davis remained in Kharpert for three years, until April of 1917, at which time the US involvement in World War I as an adversary of Turkey forced him to leave. The compound of the US Consul was located in Mezre, today's Elazig, which is at the foot of the hill upon which the town of Kharpert was located.

Davis became an eyewitness to the events of 1915, which he characterized as "probably the most terrible tragedy that has ever befallen any people in the history of the world." During his tenure as the chief US diplomat here, Davis used his compound to give shelter to hundreds of Armenians. He thereby saved hundreds of lives. He also served as a neutral American witness to the atrocities of 1915-1917.

Davis prepared numerous reports about the massacres for the US Dept. of State. His reports were filed contemporaneously with the events that he described, and were based upon his eyewitness observations. These official US documents were later published as a book titled *The Slaughterhouse Province*. For his efforts, Davis is one of the heroes of the Armenian people.

Population

Writing in 1893, H. F. B. Lynch estimated that the population of "this ancient Armenian borough" of Kharpert was between 13,000 and 25,000. Armenians made up the preponderance of the inhabitants of the surrounding region.

According to a census conducted by the Armenian Patriarchate 20 years later, in 1912, the population throughout the region consisted of a plurality of Armenians. The Patriarchate recorded 168,000 Armenians, 102,000 Turks, and 95,000 Kurds. Other population tallies by Turkish authorities from this era show fewer Armenians, and more Turks and Kurds.

VISITING KHARPERT TODAY

Depending upon your perspective, the historic Armenian town of Kharpert is located either at the summit of a small mountain, or at the top of a large hill. In either case, the site overlooks the modern city of Elazig. Kharpert is today known in Turkey as Harpoot.

The **Fortress of Kharpert** is the commanding structure of the region. The monument dates back to the medieval period, and a citadel may have existed at this site even prior to the Urartian period, in the eleventh and twelfth centuries BC. The fortress was reconstructed many times, starting with a major rebuilding by the Armenian kings of Sophene and continuing through the nineteenth century. The ruins of an Armenian church are present on the hillside near the fortress.

There's an old home from the early 1800s near the fortress that has been refurbished and outfitted in the style of a nineteenth century home, and which has opened as a **house museum**. The curators of the museum don't say this, but Kharpert's prominent Armenian families just one century ago may have lived in homes such as this one. The museum is called the **Harpoot Cefik Gul Community Center of Culture**.

The **Monastery of Khulavank** is located a short distance west of Kharpert in the village of Khoulakyugh. The village was once known as Hulvenk, and is today known by its Turkish name, Shahinkaya. According to a widely cited legend, the Apostle Thaddeus is the founder of Khulavank Monastery. The earliest

The Monastery of Tadem

physical evidence for the date of Khulavank's construction is an inscription on a wall of the church doorway that indicates it was renovated in 1301.

This was an important pilgrimage site for Armenians until 1915. When I visited the site it was abandoned and showed signs of recent vandalism. Treasure hunters had excavated the floors of the church in search of the gold that they believe Armenians concealed in their churches.

The foundation stones of other structures are located a short distance from the ruined church. These stones may be the remains of the monastery's hostel, monk cells, and orphanage building.

To get there, travel about four kilometers west of Elazig. **GPS map coordinates** for Khulavank: 38° 41' 42.24" N 39° 9' 14.51" E

Vandalism at the Monastery of Khulavank

The **Monastery of Tadem** is also nearby, south of Kharpert and just west of Lake Goljuk. The monastery is located in the village of Yalniz and is also believed to have been founded by the Apostle Thaddeus. Tadem may also have been the seat of a bishop during the seventh century.

Tadem, as was Khulavank, was an important destination for pilgrims prior to 1915. The monastery had significant holdings of land, and had jurisdiction over nine surrounding Armenian villages. Tadem today has a primitive appearance. This is because it has been almost completely stripped of its stone façade. All that remains is the rough stone core of its walls and dome.

The church dome was still intact when I visited, and was placed on a wide and short drum. These, too, had been stripped of their stone façade, so that only the rough-hewn stone blocks remain. One of the interior columns supporting the roof had been scored, so that the column, and the roof, was at risk of collapse. The floors had also been excavated, presumably by treasure hunters who believed there might be gold beneath the foundation of the church.

To get there, travel about seven kilometers south of Elazig. **GPS map coordinates** for Tadem: 38° 36' 24.49" N 39° 10' 3.31" E

The **Monastery of Soorp Nishan** was located on a small island in Lake Goljuk. This island is known as Yilan Adasi, or Snake Island and is located directly across from the former Armenian village of Goljuk, which was one of the lake's two villages in 1915.

Until about 200 years ago the island had been a peninsula. The rising level of the lake water flooded much of the land and forced the abandonment of the site as a functioning monastery sometime in the 1800s. Today, ruins from the monastery have survived but visiting the site is difficult because of its island location.

US Consul Leslie A. Davis made note of the lake in 1917 in his classified report to the US Dept. of State. Davis reported that some Armenians had used the island as a refuge in 1915, but that they were eventually captured and killed. Davis's report was declassified in 1987.

LAKE GOLJUK

One hundred years ago, when a distance was judged by the time it took to walk there, it was said that Lake Goljuk was a one-day journey from Kharpert.

There were two villages on opposite shores of the lake in 1915. One was Armenian, and one Kurdish. The rest of the shoreline was unpopulated. This was a remote destination in the deep interior of a province that was unknown to the world. The story of what happened here one hundred years ago is told in the documentary film *Voices from the Lake: The Secret Genocide*.

Long before that film was made, back in 1915, the US Consul to Kharpert Leslie A. Davis had visited Lake Goljuk to see for himself what was going on. He had heard accounts of atrocities so numerous and unimaginable that he was compelled to check their veracity.

Davis set out for the lake on horseback one morning at four o'clock, well before dawn. He had left early so that he could avoid being noticed by the Turkish authorities, whom he thought might want to stop him, or cause trouble.

After reaching the lake, Davis rode north along its banks for about two hours.

He noted that at the start of this journey that "[t] he banks of the lake for most of this distance are high and steep, while at frequent intervals there are deep valleys almost like pockets.

"In most of these valleys there are dead bodies and from the tops of the cliffs which extended between them we saw hundreds of bodies and many bones in the water below.

"It was rumored that many of the people who were brought here had been pushed over the cliffs by the gendarmes and killed in that way. That rumor was fully confirmed by what we saw. In some of the valleys there were only a few bodies, but in others there were more than a thousand."

Davis made a second trip to the lake a few weeks later, accompanied by a physician from Kharpert's American Hospital. During this trip, the pair rode to the Armenian village of Goljuk, which he described as deserted. This physician, Dr. Atkinson, estimated that he saw between 5,000 and 10,000 dead bodies at the lake during that journey.

Davis wrote a report on his observations shortly after his return to the US in 1917. He filed the report with the US Dept. of State. That report was finally declassified by the US government in 1987, and was published in 1989 in a book, *The Slaughterhouse Province*, edited by Susan K. Blair.

Davis's published reports were described shortly thereafter by the New York *Times* as "the only eyewitness account by a neutral observer of the massacres of hundreds of thousands of Armenians."

If you travel to Lake Goljuk, which is today known in Turkey as Lake Hazar, you will see sandy beaches, and clear water. You will see picnic areas, and vacation homes. The evidence of what had happened here a century ago appears to have been washed away. But if you will recall Hagopian's film, and Davis's report, you will understand that the evidence from Lake Goljuk will last forever.

Egin / Akn

The town of **Egin** (also known to Armenians as **Akn** or **Agn**) was a prominent Armenian town located northwest of Kharpert. The town is today known in Turkey by the name Kemaliye. Egin is the Armenian word for spring, and the town apparently took this name because of a large source of nearby water that allowed the village to develop.

Egin was home to about 19,000 people just before 1915, and had become a significant center of activity as early as 1830. Some accounts report that migrants from Van originally settled Egin as early as the eleventh century.

By the 1890s, Egin was roaring with activity. The town was served by 20 banks and supported a significant amount of light industry, including furriers, tanneries, and textiles. This was a prosperous town, as evidenced by its support for two Armenian churches, and seven Armenian schools, as well as by its ability to sustain so much commercial activity.

An orphanage, set up by American missionaries, was operated here shortly after 1895 to address the needs of the many Armenian children of Egin whose parents had been murdered. Some of the children at the orphanage were taught the craft of rug making and their woven rugs were offered for sale. Rug weaving was a desirable trade for Armenian orphans 100 years ago. The **Ghazir Rug**, which was woven in Lebanon by the children of genocide victims and donated in 1925 to US President Coolidge, is perhaps the most famous of these so-called "orphan rugs."

Holy Trinity Armenian Church, Malatya

Malatya

The city of **Malatya**, which is widely known for its bountiful harvest of sweet apricots, but which is better known to Armenians as the birthplace of the human rights activist and journalist **Hrant Dink**, had a significant Armenian population until 1915.

Most of the Armenians of Malatya had lived in the city, rather than in villages, and the neighborhood of **Cavusoglu** became known as the city's Armenian Quarter. Here in the **Armenian Quarter**, the **Holy Trinity Armenian Church** has survived the past century and was undergoing rehabilitation, funded by local Armenians, in 2014.

A handful of Armenians still live in the Cavusoglu neighborhood that surrounds this church. During my visit to the area, I was invited into the home of an Armenian who lived down the street from the church with her husband, a Christian from Syria. Her mother survived the genocide, and she lives openly as a Christian Armenian in this once-thriving Armenian neighborhood.

The childhood home of Hrant Dink was in this area, as well, and there has been some discussion recently about naming a street in his honor.

The church of **Soorp Grigor Lusavorich (St. Gregory the Illuminator)**, located about seven kilometers from the center of Malatya, has been recently reconstructed. The structure, on a hill overlooking the city, is now similar in appearance to a bunker. Most pilgrims will find this site to be uninspiring.

Houshamadyan

The non-profit Houshamadyan Association studies the social history and anthropology of the Armenians of Western Armenia. Their website is a good resource for information about the lives that Armenians led in the villages and towns of Western Armenia 100 years ago.

Visit the website at www.Houshamadyan.org

Home in the former Armenian district of Sebastia (now Sivas)

Sebastia

INTRODUCTION

Sebastia is the heart of the region known as **Lesser Armenia**, or **Pokr Hayk**. This is the westernmost of the historic Armenian territories, and includes the important towns of Sebastia, **Marsovan**, and **Gurun**, as well as the *sanjak* (county) of **Shabin-Karahisar**.

Throughout the region, the population and culture here was more mixed than in other parts of Armenia, and produced an abundant share of Armenian poets, artists, craftsmen, and political leaders. The region and its provincial center are today both known as Sivas.

Few monuments remain in Sebastia to attest to the Armenian heritage of the region. The most prominent monument, the **Monastery of Soorp Nishan (The Monastery of the Holy Cross)**, which was located just outside the city of Sebastia, was abandoned in 1915 and then destroyed in 1980 by the Turkish army. It had been established in the early eleventh century.

Soorp Nishan had a library that contained a collection of medieval Armenian manuscripts. The library was not destroyed in 1915, and most of the manuscripts survived long enough for them to be rescued and moved to either the Matenadaran in Yerevan or to the Armenian Patriarchate in Jerusalem.

The Turkish army built a military depot on the site of the monastery as early as 1939, and used the site as a military base sometime after this. The army is believed to have started demolishing the monastery in 1978, a process that continued at least until 1980. Nothing remains of this thousand year old monastery today.

There were at least forty other churches and monasteries in the Sebastia area prior to 1915. Throughout the entire Sivas region there may have been as many as 198 churches and 21 monasteries, according to some sources. They have all been either destroyed, or converted to other uses and significantly altered.

For the past century, the **Soorp Kevork Armenian Church**, located just outside Sivas, was thought to be one of these many churches that had been destroyed, or reconfigured as something unrecognizable. The church had been sequestered in a military zone since 1940. In 2013 the Turkish army announced that the church was still standing, and that the army would give the church to an organization known as the Friends of Armenians Association of Sivas.

Within the city of Sivas in 1915 there were at least four, and perhaps as many as six, Armenian Apostolic churches, as well as an Armenian Protestant and an Armenian Catholic church. None of them is standing today.

Soorp Nishan is widely known as the monastery at which **Mkhitar Sebastatsi** studied as a monk. Mkhitar Sebastatsi was born in 1676 and founded the organization that would become known after his death as the **Mkhitarist Order** at San Lazzaro, Italy.

An Armenian pilgrim visiting Sivas today will find that almost everything Armenian has been destroyed. According to Christina Maranci, the scholar and expert on Armenian architecture, "the art and architecture of Armenians in Sebastia must [instead] be conjured up through the historical imagination."

VISITING SEBASTIA TODAY

A former Armenian school building occupies a prominent location in the heart of today's **Sivas**, the city known to Armenians as historic **Sebastia**. The building, which was erected in 1892, was later taken by the Turkish government and was used in 1919 as the Sivas Congress, Turkey's first national congress.

The ruins of Armenian homes, some with keystones still in place, attest to the Armenian heritage of Sebastia, and are still scattered about the city. Apart from these, there are no prominent historic Armenian monuments remaining in the city.

Almost every indication of Armenian Sebastia located within the city limits of Sivas has been erased since 1915. Pilgrims searching for Armenian Sebastia will have greater success outside the city.

Soorp Kevork, an Armenian church located on a Turkish military base just outside Sivas, was still off-limits at time of research, but the plan of the Turkish army to donate the building to a local Armenian group suggests that this might be a site that will soon be on the list for Armenian pilgrimages.

Soorp Astvatsatsin Church, Gurun

A news report in 2013 suggested that the structure of the church might be in good condition. The reason? When the military seized the building and the surrounding land for an army base back in 1940, the church became inaccessible to treasure hunters who might otherwise have dug up the foundation looking for gold. The walls and roof of the church are both intact.

Gurun was the main provincial town in the *sanjak* (county) of the same name, which is located south of Sivas. This was once a predominantly Armenian town. Fifteen thousand people lived here just before 1915. Two thirds of them were Armenian.

The town had been well known at that time for its manufacture of woven shawls, which were reputed to be the best, and the most attractive, of any produced in the Armenian provinces. The first mechanized loom in the Armenian provinces was said to be the one that was brought here from England by an Armenian of Gurun, Sarkis Minassian.

The industry was wiped out in 1915. The shawls of Gurun, once available at fine shops, must now be viewed instead at places such as the Sivas Museum of Antiquities.

The municipality of Gurun is today restoring some of the old Armenian homes that are now occupied by Kurds and Turks. Not everything is being restored. On one old portal, I observed a missing keystone—the keystone that in 1915 would have been inscribed in Armenian with the name of the family who lived there.

Gurun's **Soorp Astvatsatsin Church (Holy Mother of God)** in the center of town is rundown, but appears to be structurally sound. The mayor of Gurun announced in 2013 that the municipality planned to restore the church and turn it into a museum and cultural center. The church was erected in the 1800s, and for a time following 1915 it had been used as a jail, a cinema, and a store.

Govdun, a village about 20 kilometers east of Sebastia, still has the remains of its old Armenian church, **Soorp Karapet (Garabed)**, which is today used as a barn. There were about 250 to 300 Armenian families living here just before 1915, and the population was about 3,000.

The village is celebrated as the birthplace, in 1872, of Murad Hagopian, the Armenian freedom fighter who would later became known as simply **Sebastatsi Murad**. He was killed in battle at Baku in 1918 while defending the city against the advancing Turkish army.

Zara, located roughly 70 kilometers east of Sivas, was a mixed Armenian and Muslim town just prior to 1915, and today one can still view the remnants of an Armenian cemetery, and the ruins of the century-old Armenian district. After a century of neglect, only one Armenian tombstone remained standing. Many of the rest appear to have been plundered.

Today's Zara has a population of about 12,000 people, most of whom are Turkish. During my research in Zara I encountered a young man who identified himself and his brother as the Last Armenians of Zara. If there are others, then they have concealed their identities.

Prknig was the birthplace in 1884 of **Daniel Varoujan**, and he lived in this small village until he was 12 years old. Varoujan is esteemed as one of Armenia's greatest poets. He was working as the principal of an Armenian school in Istanbul in 1915 when he was arrested during the mass arrests of April 24. He was murdered shortly afterward.

The large county of **Shabin-Karahisar**, in northern Sebastia, is famous for its role resisting the deportations and massacres of 1915. The resistance at Shabin-Karahisar lasted from June 16 through July 12, 1915.

By July 13 the entire Armenian population of Shabin-Karahisar had been massacred. By this time, it was apparent that it was the plan of the Ottoman government to have an "Armenia without Armenians," according to a statement written on that day by the Armenian Patriarch of Istanbul.

One month later, the New York *Times* reported the massacre of the Armenians of Shabin-Karahisar. On August 18, 1915 the *Times* carried a story bearing the headline "Armenians Are Sent to Perish in Desert, Turks Accused of Plan to Exterminate Whole Population—People of Karahisar Massacred." Shabin-Karahisar had a population of about 25,000 Armenians here just prior to 1915.

The resistance here represented one of only four significant efforts at self-defense by the Armenians during the genocide. Armenians also organized in self-defense at Van, at Musa Dagh, and at Urfa.

Shabin-Karahisar was the birthplace in 1865 of Andranik Ozanian, the Armenian leader who would become known to most Armenians as **Commander Andranik**, or more often, simply as Andranik.

Marsovan is located in the far northwest of the province of Sebastia, and was the most northwest reaching part of historic Armenia. The town was home to the Anatolia College, which was founded in the 1886, and to three Armenian churches. Today's Turkish name for the town is Merzifon.

The former Armenian district of Gurun

THE LAST ARMENIANS OF ZARA

Ahmet Komurcu is one of the last Armenians of Zara. The other two are his brother and his father.

I had met Ahmet by chance while I was traveling. I had been looking for the old Armenian quarter of Zara, and so I stopped an old man on the street and asked for directions.

"I love Armenians," the man on the street told me. I have a friend who is Armenian, "just like you," he said.

And so instead of directing me to the old Armenian quarter, he directed me to his old Armenian friend.

I arranged to meet Ahmet, the Armenian son of the old man's old Armenian friend. Ahmet was wary at first, but he quickly warmed up when he determined that I *really* was an Armenian from the US and that I really just wanted to meet another Armenian.

There's no Armenian church, or school, or Armenian community in Zara. Ahmet lives openly as an Armenian, but he says he is isolated. His wife is Muslim, and their children, he says, are Muslim, as well. Ahmet knows he is an Armenian, but he cannot practice his faith.

He took me to the Armenian district. He showed me the ruins of old Armenian homes, and the plundered Armenian cemetery. Ahmet's brother, Sinan, joined us.

Ahmet and Sinan say they know nothing of their family history beyond their conviction that they are 100 percent Armenian, born to parents who were both Armenian. They know that they are the last Armenians of Zara.

While we were at the Armenian cemetery, a visitor gave Ahmet an Armenian cross necklace. Ahmet pulled the necklace over his head. He smiled.

He had never had an Armenian cross, he said. Where would he buy one, in a town with just three Armenians? He was happy to be able to wear the one he had just received.

He was still wearing the cross when we left him—one of the town's last Armenians, wearing the town's only Armenian cross.

GETTING TO KHARPERT AND SEBASTIA

There are several flights to Elazig, Sivas, and Kayseri each day from Istanbul and Ankara. Elazig is the airport that serves visitors to Kharpert (Harpoot). Sivas is the airport that serves the region of Sebastia. Kayseri serves the region of Kesaria and Cappadocia. Frequent bus service operates through each of these towns, as well.

When to Visit

The *badarak* is performed several Sundays each year at the church of Soorp Grigor Lusavorich in Kayseri (Kesaria). One of these Sundays would be a memorable time for a visit.

Suggested Itinerary

This suggested itinerary covers the highlights of the Kharpert, Sebastia, and Cappadocia regions, in roughly the order of significance of the sites, so that you can plan a visit of from one to six days.

1. Day One: Morning at the Kharpert Fortress and the old town of Kharpert; Afternoon at the nearby Monasteries of Khulavank and Tadem.

2. Day Two: Travel to Malatya; Afternoon at the Armenian Quarter of Malatya.

3. Day Three: Morning in Malatya; afternoon and sunset at Nemrut Dagi.

4. Day Four: Travel west to Gurun; late morning at Gurun and then continue north to Sivas.

5. Day Five: Morning in the city of Sivas. Depart for Kayseri (Kesaria) in afternoon.

6. Day Six: Morning in the city of Kayseri's Armenian district and at its two surviving Armenian churches; afternoon in nearby Talas.

The portal to a former Armenian home in Gurun, as seen in 2014.
A stone above the entrance to Armenian homes frequently bore the name of the
family living there. The stone above this door is conspicuous by its absence.

Visiting Historic Armenia

Getting There

If you plan to travel to historic Armenia from North America, the easiest way to get there is by flying into Istanbul and then connecting on a domestic flight to eastern Turkey. Turkish Airlines offers direct flights, some of them non-stop, from Los Angeles and New York to Istanbul and Ankara.

After arriving in Istanbul or Ankara, it is a simple matter to connect on a Turkish Airlines flight to your destination. Turkish Airlines offers daily flights, sometimes several each day, between Istanbul and the following cities: Kars, Van, Igdir, Erzerum, Mush, Diyarbakir, Elazig (Kharpert), Sivas (Sebastia), Malatya, and Kayseri (Kesaria).

The land border between Armenia and Turkey has been closed for more than two decades, so if you plan to visit both countries, or if you plan to travel to Turkey from Armenia, you will need to use Georgia as a point of transit. There may sometimes be flights between Yerevan and Istanbul, once per week, but these are subject to interruption and cannot be relied upon.

Safety

The Turkish authorities do not appear to discriminate unfairly against tourists who have Armenian surnames. There also does not appear to be any bias against tourists with Armenian passports, or who have visas in their passports that have been issued by Armenia or by Karabakh (Artsakh).

Some private businesses have been known to refuse service to Armenians or to visitors who identify themselves as Armenian. This is not a common occurrence in eastern Turkey, where the population is predominantly Kurdish. In Istanbul, and in western Turkey where the population is mostly Turkish, there may be greater anti-Armenian sentiment. Armenian travelers are advised to be cautious when discussing their ethnicity with strangers.

There was no civil unrest in the eastern provinces at time of research, and no safety reason for anyone to avoid traveling to Ani, Kars, Van, Bitlis, and Mush. Travelers to Diyarbakir, however, should beware of pickpockets and should avoid walking alone in the city's many alleys.

Travelers should avoid the region of Turkey that borders directly on Iraq and Syria because of the risk that the unrest in those two countries could affect the adjacent regions of Turkey. Conditions change over time, however, and readers are advised to carefully evaluate the risks of travel before planning a trip to the region.

Getting Around

Turkish Airlines uses Istanbul and Ankara as its only hubs. This will usually be inconvenient for air travelers and will cause you to lose valuable time. Instead, travel between the cities of eastern Turkey by bus.

Turkey's bus lines are modern, clean, and comfortable. Buses are the best method of public transportation for traveling between any of the cities in the east. Take flights only when traveling in or out of Istanbul or Ankara.

Within cities, and in between villages and small towns, using public transportation may be cumbersome. Mini-vans, known locally as the dolmus, operate within many towns and are cheap, but can be time consuming. Taxis can be very costly. Car rentals are an affordable option, especially in areas such as Kars and Van, where traveling to many distant sites will require private transportation.

Visa

Most visitors, including visitors from the US, need a visa to gain entry to Turkey. This visa should be obtained before you arrive at Istanbul, by applying online for an electronic visa. Your passport must be valid for six months beyond the date of your departure from Turkey.

Lodging

Accommodations can be rudimentary in many parts of eastern Turkey. Tourist class facilities nevertheless exist in all of the major cities. For the best accommodations, plan to stay in the provincial capitals, rather than in smaller towns. There are clean and modern hotels available in all of the cities that have commercial airports, including Kars, Van, Igdir, Mush, Diyarbakir, Elazig (near Kharpert), Malatya, Erzerum, Erzincan (Erzinjan), and Sivas (Sebastia).

References

Ambassador Morgenthau's Story, Henry Morgenthau (Doubleday Books, 1919).

Armenia: A Historical Atlas, Robert Hewsen (University of Chicago Press, 2001).

Armenia and Karabakh: The Stone Garden Travel Guide, Matthew Karanian (Stone Garden Productions, 2013).

Armenia on Horseback, George Hepworth (E. P. Dutton and Co., 1898).

Armenian Baghesh/Bitlis and Taron/Mush, Richard G. Hovannisian, ed. (Mazda Publishers, 2001).

Armenian Karin/Erzerum, Richard G. Hovannisian, ed. (Mazda Publishers, 2003).

Armenian Kars and Ani, Richard G. Hovannisian, ed. (Mazda Publishers, 2011).

Armenian Sebastia/Sivas and Lesser Armenia, Richard G. Hovannisian, ed. (Mazda Publishers, 2004).

Armenian Tigranakert/Diarbekir and Edessa/Urfa, Richard G. Hovannisian, ed. (Mazda Publishers, 2006).

Armenian Tsopk/Kharpert, Richard G. Hovannisian, ed. (Mazda Publishers, 2002).

Armenian Van/Vaspurakan, Richard G. Hovannisian, ed. (Mazda Publishers, 2000).

An American Physician in Turkey, Clarence D. Usher (Houghton Mifflin Co., 1917).

Armenia: A Year at Erzeroom, and on the Frontiers of Russia, Turkey, and Persia, Robert Curzon (Harper & Brothers, 1854).

Armenia: Travels and Studies, Vols. I-II, H. F. B. Lynch (Khayat Book and Publishing Co., 1965)

Armenian Golgatha, Grigoris Balakian (Vintage Books, 2010).

Armenians in Diyarbekir Province, Osman Koker, ed. (Birzamanlar Yayincilik, 2011).

The Burning Tigris, Peter Balakian (Harper Perennial, 2004).

Children of Armenia: A Forgotten Genocide and the Century-Long Struggle for Justice, Michael Bobelian (Simon and Schuster, 2012).

The Crossing Place, Philip Marsden (Harper Collins, 1993).

Days of Tragedy in Armenia: Personal Experiences in Harpoot, 1915-1917, Henry H. Riggs (Gomidas Institute, 1997).

The Defense of Van, Onnig Mikhitarian and Haig Gossoian (Raven Publishers, 1980).

Documents of Armenian Architecture (Levon Azarian, Armen Manoukian, editors) Aght'amar (Vo. 8) 1974; Ani (Vol. 12) 1984.

History of the Armenian Genocide: Ethnic Conflict from the Balkans to Anatolia to the Caucasus, Vahakn N. Dadrian (Berghahn Books, 1995).

Marsovan 1915: The Diaries of Bertha Morley, Bertha B. Morley (Taderon Press, 2000).

A Shameful Act: The Armenian Genocide and the Question of Turkish Responsibility, Taner Akcam (Henry Holt and Co., 2006).

The Slaughterhouse Province: An American Diplomat's Report on the Armenian Genocide, 1915-1917, Leslie A. Davis, Susan K. Blair, ed. (A. D. Caratzas, 1989).

The Survival of a Nation, Christopher Walker (St. Martin's Press, 1980).

The Tragedy of Bitlis, Grace H. Knapp (Fleming H. Revell Co., 1919).

FILM AND VIDEO

Orphans of the Genocide, Directed by Bared Maronian, Armenoid Productions, Coconut Creek, Florida 2010.

Voices from the Lake: A Film about the Secret Genocide, Directed by J. Michael Hagopian. Armenian Film Foundation, Thousand Oaks, California 2000.

Acknowledgements

I am thankful to **Khatchig Mouradian, Ph D**, for his assistance during the research and production of this book. Khatchig introduced me to many historic sites in Western Armenia, including important places such as Palu and Chunkush, and others too numerous to mention. He served as my bridge to the hidden Armenians of the region. Khatchig's advocacy on behalf of Armenians, as both a scholar and as a journalist, helped me to appreciate the importance of this book.

George Aghayan proved himself to be a worthy navigator during my research trips to Western Armenia. Thank you, George, for sharing your knowledge of the homeland, and also for finding the GPS coordinates that helped us locate so many forgotten treasures, such as the forgotten Tzarakar Monastery, in the region of Kars. Without your expertise, and your passion for exploration, many important sites would certainly have gone unvisited.

I am also grateful to **Armen Aroyan** for providing valuable research about historic sites throughout Western Armenia, including in towns such as Zara and Gurun, which are both in the Sebastia region, and in Erzincan, which is in the region of Erzerum.

The scholar of Armenian history **Prof. Robert H. Hewsen** labored for two decades to create "Armenia: A Historical Atlas," a brilliant and exhaustively detailed cartographical history of Armenia. He generously allowed several of the maps from his Atlas to be printed in this book— an extraordinary gift of his knowledge and scholarship.

Dr. Rouben Adalian of the Armenian National Institute provided an important historic photograph that shows a scene from the 1915 deportations. Thanks also to Prof. **Peter Balakian** for his counsel and advice, and to **Aren Kurkjian** for proofreading the final manuscript.

I was able to include several 100-year old photographs in this book thanks to the generosity of **John Donelian**, **Vahe Tachjian**, and **Samvel Karapetyan**. John Donelian supplied a set of antique photographs that were created a century ago by the photographer Vartan Hampikian. Vahe Tachjian of the Houshamadyan Project also made many images available. Samvel Karapetyan of the Research on Armenian Architecture Foundation provided the 100-year old image of Khtzkonk Monastery.

Thank you, most of all, to my two greatest supporters: my parents **Henry** and **Agnes Karanian**. Without their support, none of this would have been possible, and even less would have been important. My parents were both born in the US. Each of them was the first American-born child in their family—a privilege that never cast a shadow over their Western Armenian roots.

My father died in 2008, several years before this publication. His role in the creation of this book was nevertheless as palpable as was the role of my mother, who, at age 90, actively supported this project, going so far as to read two early drafts of the book and to offer many constructive comments. This book is a manifestation of my great respect and admiration for my parents.

The genesis of this book, however, must certainly have been my grandparents. The story of their survival, and their resilience, is a story that is at once both unique to their lives and also shared by so many Armenian families—a common thread in the fabric of Armenian history.

Dad's mother **Ardemis** (1904-2000) was a survivor from Marsovan, a large town in Western Armenia. She was a 15 year old *orphan of the genocide* who had arrived at Ellis Island with her grandmother in 1920. Dad's father **Hovhannes** (1896-1964) was a teenager from Van when his family had the prescience to send him to the US just two years before the start of the genocide.

Mom's mother **Houstian** (1888-1959) was deported in 1915 from Zara, a small town near Sebastia, also in Western Armenia. She was a *widow of the genocide* when she escaped to the US in 1922 to start life anew with her one surviving child. Mom's father **Oskean** (1885-1950) had the fortune to be able to flee Sebastia and travel to the US just one year before the genocide. Their experiences informed my parents' lives. Our shared history inspired me to create this book.

Index

173

The author during research at Ani
Photo by Talin Avakian

ABOUT THE AUTHOR / PHOTOGRAPHER

Matthew Karanian is a lawyer, writer, and photographer. He is a second generation Armenian American and the author of several books about Armenia.

Karanian first traveled to the Republic of Armenia in 1995 and to the historic lands of Western Armenia two years later, in 1997. This book is the product of the author's several research and photography trips to Ani, Kars, and the six provinces of Western Armenia between 1997 and 2014.

Some of the inspiration for Karanian's research and photography derive from his family history. His two grandmothers are survivors from the Western Armenian towns of Marsovan and Zara. They escaped to the US as refugees after 1915. The author's two grandfathers had traveled to the US shortly before 1915 from the Western Armenian towns of Van and Sebastia.

As a legal scholar, Karanian has served as Associate Dean of the law school at the American University of Armenia, where he founded the Armenian Law Review. He has also served as a Caucasus specialist in the Republic of Georgia with the Institute for the Study of International Migration, a Georgetown University research center.

Karanian has studied law in London, Salzburg, and Budapest, and he holds law degrees from Georgetown University Law Center and from McGeorge School of Law. He practices law in Los Angeles.

Karanian is also the author of *Armenia and Karabakh: The Stone Garden Travel Guide*, a best-selling guide to the Republics of Armenia and Artsakh (Karabakh), and co-author with Robert Kurkjian of *Out of Stone: Armenia-Artsakh*.